Another Place at the Table

JEREMY P. TARCHER/PUTNAM

a member of Penguin Putnam Inc.

New York

Another
Place
at
the
Table

A Story of Shattered Childhoods
Redeemed by Love

KATHY HARRISON

This is the story of my family — my birth children, my adoptive children, and the many other children who have joined our family, however briefly, over the years. My birth children and adoptive children are identified by their real first names. I have changed the names and background characteristics of my adoptive children's birth families, as well as the names and background characteristics of the many other children who have become part of our extended family. This was done out of respect for their privacy. The names of certain other people who appear in the book have also been changed.

Most Tarcher/Putnam books are available at special quantity discounts for bulk purchases for sales promotions, premiums, fund-raising, and educational needs. Special books or book excerpts also can be created to fit specific needs. For details, write Putnam Special Markets, 375 Hudson Street, New York, NY 10014.

Jeremy P. Tarcher/Putnam
a member of
Penguin Putnam Inc.
375 Hudson Street
New York, NY 10014
www.penguinputnam.com

Library of Congress Cataloging-in-Publication Data

Harrison, Kathryn, date.
Another place at the table: a story of shattered childhoods
redeemed by love / by Kathy Harrison.
p. cm.
ISBN 1-58542-200-2
1. Harrison, Kathryn, date. 2. Foster home care—Massachusetts—Case studies. 3. Foster mothers—Massachusetts—
Biography. 4. Foster children—Massachusetts—Biography.
I. Title.
HV883.M4 H37   2003   2002028707
362.73'3'092—dc21

Printed in the United States of America
1   3   5   7   9   10   8   6   4   2

This book is printed on acid-free paper. ∞

This book is dedicated to my many families.

My husband, Bruce, and our children, Bruce Jr., Nathan, Benjamin, Neddy, Angie, and Karen, provided the love and support that made our odd family possible.

My sister and brothers, Gloria Williams, Robert Scott, and James Scott, are a constant reminder of the importance of a shared history.

My mother, Jean Scott, always knew I could.

The children who came to us, alone and afraid, never arrived without a story that needed to be told and never left without taking a piece of our hearts with them.

Another Place at the Table

Introduction

Given the life I have chosen to lead, I have come to dread that moment in cocktail party conversation when somebody asks the inevitable question "What do you do?" I envy my husband's easy answer. Bruce is the director of building services for a large extended-care facility. Managing staff and budgets and projects falls within a framework of experience that most people can understand. My response is a bit more difficult. For the past thirteen years, I have been a foster mom.

Foster parenting conjures up different images for different people. Some folks hear my answer, smile politely, and move on, seeing only a woman who spends her time watching *Sesame Street* and changing diapers. Others launch into a tirade on the evils of the system, viewing me as a part of it. Most seem genuinely puzzled by what exactly such a life might be like. I have no easy answer. Even for me, with the voices of nearly one hundred children whispering in my ear, the reality changes from day to day. There are times when it seems like what I mostly do is wash. Dishes and floors, faces and mismatched socks—I take the dirty and make it clean. Other days it seems like I do so much more. When children come to me they are shattered. In the course of a few short hours they have lost everything that anchored them to their sense of self.

They are truly refuges from a war they can't begin to comprehend. My job is to paste them together until they can start to make some sense of it all. I offer a small island of safety in an unsafe and terrifying world.

This is not an easy picture to paint for a stranger, nor is it the one I envisioned painting for myself. Bruce and I grew up only a few miles from each other in the small hill towns of western Massachusetts. We married young and quickly set about the business of raising a family. Our three sons were a joy to us. We spent their early years on a lovely old farm that was part of a privately owned historical preservation project. We made very little money, but there were compensations. Our sons, Bruce, Nathan, and Ben, recall a rather idyllic childhood of milking cows and chasing chickens. We grew most of what we ate and relied on our church and community for outside entertainment: It was an insulated life. We didn't get television reception, so we were shielded from even vicarious exposure to the outside world.

All that changed in 1988. Bruce had built up a considerable reputation in facility management. He was offered a job with an attractive salary in the health care industry just as we began to think about a future that would include college tuition. Although it meant moving off of the farm, he took the job, and, for the first time since the boys were born, I was faced with the prospect of finding both a house and gainful employment.

We knew we wanted to stay in the same small town our boys had been born in. There was much to recommend it. It was small and safe, and the schools were excellent. It was the kind of community that still hosted potluck dinners, Sunday afternoon baseball games, and town picnics in the park. It just felt like home.

The late eighties saw the tail end of the real estate boom. There was little suburban housing to be found in our price range. We ended up paying too much for a place that was far too big and run-down for a middle-aged couple with three kids. It was a drafty old barn of a place, decorated in a sixties' version of bad taste. Everything was painted a hideous chocolate brown except the bathroom. For some inexplicable reason, the walls in there had been shingled. The plumber we called refused to touch the pipes, although he did spend a profitable half hour in the cellar shaking his head and muttering. When the electrician and heating contractor had the same reaction to the wiring and the furnace we began to worry that our original renovation estimates were off by several years and more money than we cared to think about. Still, there was enough land for a garden, and we set to work with more enthusiasm than good sense.

Finding a job proved to be easier than I expected. I had taken enough courses in early childhood education over the years to apply for my certificate to teach and quickly landed a job working with at-risk four-year-olds in a local Head Start program. Working in Head Start was an eye-opening experience. The Head Start kids were not the carefree, well-tended children I was accustomed to. Six of the eighteen children in the program lived in foster homes. Many had been exposed to violence far beyond anything in my experience. Some were tough, some were wary, but each managed to touch me in a way that was both intoxicating and unexpected.

I found myself intrigued by the foster families. Some were very good, some frightenly bad. Money and education had nothing to do with how loving and responsive a family was. Some of the really good homes teetered on the very edge of poverty, but they had an intangible something in common, an aura of openness and warmth that drew me as surely as it drew the children. For the first time I felt a stir of a calling. I wondered if this was who I was or who I could be.

My own family has a long history of social service. Some of my earliest memories involve finding an extra person or two, and sometimes entire families, sitting at the dinner table. Both of my parents had a habit of bringing home folks who were a bit down on their luck for a meal and a safe place to sleep. In the early 1960s, when it was still common practice to disown daughters who found themselves pregnant without the benefit of marriage, my parents opened their doors to several single soon-to-be-mothers. Their legacy of service was passed on to all four of their children.

Given that history, it was no surprise that I found myself drawn to the foster children in my program. One child in particular spoke to me. Angelica was as different from my sons as it was possible to be. Whereas they were fair and lanky, *Mayflower* roots clear in every facial plane, Angelica was a Latino beauty, dark and sturdy, with an air of self-reliance unusual in one so young. Her foster home had little to offer her. Angie, in her foster parents' opinion, was a troublemaker and not at all interested in changing her street-smart behavior in order to fit in. Toward the end of the school year, it became clear that her behavior in her foster home had deteriorated to the point that continued placement there was in no one's best interest.

Bruce and I discussed her predicament many nights as we watched our three happy, secure boys play ball in the backyard. Bruce, of course, had never met Angie, so I would have understood if he hadn't been able to worry about her with the same intensity as someone who spent five days a week with her, but that's not who Bruce is. Once he heard her story he was as concerned as I about a four-year-old child, alone in the world, with no one to care where she laid her head each night. Angie's mother was drug addicted and in poor health. It was unlikely that she could ever assume the full-time care of her daughter. The question was, Could we?

I'm not sure when "can we" changed to "how can we" and then to "how can we not", but over the course of a few weeks, it did. We talked to the boys, took the state-mandated, thirty-hour training program required of all foster and adoptive parents, and brought Angie home. Six months later, Angie's eight-year-old sister, Neddy, joined us, and our family felt complete.

Now, in our particular circle of friends, two children were the norm, three a bit excessive, and five simply unheard of. But five was what we had, and, by anyone's standards, five should have been enough.

Social services, however, did not see it that way. The problem was one of a perpetual shortage of qualified foster homes. Homes that were willing to take out-of-control teens or hyperactive toddlers are always full. Fewer stay-at-home parents means fewer places available for newborns or medically needy children. With beds in such short supply, it is no wonder that because we had a training certificate in hand and a couple of empty bedrooms, our phone started ringing with requests that we take Juanita or Thomas or Kellie "just for a few days."

In the beginning, it was easy to say no. Bruce and I were in the process of adopting Angie and Neddy, and we really didn't want to be foster parents. We had only taken the training and gotten our certificate because it was required of us before we could pursue adopting the girls. We worried that the comings and goings of other needy children would make our girls wonder about our long-term commitment to them.

After several months, though, my resistance began to crumble. It wasn't that I wanted or needed any more children. It was just that every story was so darn sad, and I always did suffer from an overactive imagination. It wasn't much of a leap for me to turn a nameless, sexually abused six-year-old into a real little girl. I knew how her unwashed body would smell. I could see her feet dangle as she shifted uncomfortably in the hard plastic chairs of the holding area where at-risk children wait as they are processed through the Massachusetts Department of Social Services. I could feel her sitting there, waiting for someone, anyone, to want her. Would anyone feed her? Would anyone have time to sit with her or hold her hand?

I knew that office. It was filled with kind, well-intentioned people who were busy putting out fires. They wouldn't have time to do much for this child but give her a warm Coke and a quick pat on the head before they rushed off to the next emergency.

What a girl like this needed, I had. She needed some uninterrupted time with a grown-up who cared about who she was, one who could guess what it felt like to be her. She needed a bath and clean sheets, and she needed to feel safe for a bit. I could do that. We could all move over a little and squeeze her in.

So I took in Madeleine, then Gabrielle, and then Tyrone.

Now, a full-time job with five children is one thing, but a full-time job with eight children is quite another. Even with everyone pitching in, after a year the stress began to tell on all of us. There wasn't enough of either Bruce or me to go around. We needed to make a family decision. Either we stopped doing foster care and I kept my job or we made a commitment to foster and I would hand in my resignation to Head Start.

It was a tough call and not one made any easier by the ambivalence Bruce and I shared about the social service system. Living with our daughters gave us some firsthand experience with what the pain of losing a family is like for children. We held the girls each night as they sobbed in anguish over that loss. As much as we loved them, we couldn't help but wish there had been another, less painful option than foster care for them when their birth mothers couldn't cope. It felt odd to choose to entangle ourselves in a system that, despite its honorable intentions, often seemed to do as much harm as good. I found it difficult to even identify myself as a foster parent. The press was so bad and often seemed so well deserved. Still, my good times outweighed my bad, and, child by child, I learned just how important a safe haven could be.

Much has changed since that moment, thirteen years ago, when Angie walked in our front door with all her belongings in a green plastic trash bag. I never returned to my classroom. Instead, I chose to devote myself to caring for the state's neediest children. I have fostered abandoned babies and runaway teens; preschoolers in wheelchairs and ten-year-old girls just discharged from psychiatric hospitals.

Our boys have become men. Today, young Bruce is a devoted father. Nathan is a counselor for disturbed adolescent boys. Ben is taking two years off from college to do missionary work in California. Our daughters are young women. They have discovered talents in sports and music: The bookcase in the den sags with the weight of a dozen years' worth of trophies and commendations.

They are both attending a private women's college and call nearly every day to touch base. They have bloomed, though the roots of their early insecurity run deep.

We have another daughter now. Karen came to us in infancy as a foster child. We adopted her when she was three. She was the perfect child—healthy, bright, and beautiful. But when Karen turned four, we began to notice some neurological problems. At five, our little girl was diagnosed with Tourette's syndrome. At six, she developed obsessive-compulsive disorder and, at seven, early-onset bipolar disorder. We have learned that perfect is all about perception. While Bruce and I, along with Karen's brothers and sisters, grieve the loss of the easy childhood we envisioned for her, we celebrate the strength and courage and resilience that Karen possesses. I am grateful every day for the joy my daughter brings to me.

Bruce and I have changed too. I know that I am slower to panic but quicker to anger, especially if I think that someone is not doing his or her job and one of my kids is suffering because of it. I'm less intimidated by people in positions of authority. I have learned the hard way that "well educated" doesn't always mean "smart." I am more aware of my limitations and better at respecting them. I say no to requests more often than I say yes, and I no longer agonize or apologize when I do. Every child will fit someplace, but that place isn't always here. For his part, Bruce is now much more involved in the decision-making process than he used to be.

Living in a family with a constantly shifting cast of characters is challenging at best. I don't accept a child any more without first running his or her history and behaviors by Bruce. Together we decide whether this looks like something we can handle without adversely affecting Karen. We have learned that, in spite of our best intentions, we can't save everybody. And we take better care of each other. After Karen's diagnosis, we designed a sanctuary in the backyard. We spend time there every day, weather permitting, to connect and reflect.

This is such hard-earned wisdom. It comes with a price tag I could never have anticipated when I began. The price is paid in installments, by my husband and by our children, every time we love and lose and every time we can't love enough. Mostly, though, it is paid by the children who knock at my door.

This is the story of a number of children who touched my life, but primarily it is the story of Danny, Sara, Lucy, and Karen. They came together in my home, and nothing was ever quite the same after. Although their stories are horrifying, what stands out about them is that they are not unique at all. There are over a half-million children in foster care in the United States. In Massachusetts alone, twenty children enter care each day. Each child has a tragic history, and each has the same potential for violence or redemption.

This book is not intended to shock, although it may do that. It was not written to change public policy. I'm far too much of a realist to expect that. It is only the story of one family's journey through the maze of a social service system and of the children who unwittingly led the way.

Chapter

One

❖

C.119.1. Policy of the Commonwealth of Massachusetts

The purpose of this chapter is to insure that the children of this commonwealth are protected against the harmful effects resulting from the absence, inability, inadequacy or destructive behavior of parents or parent substitutes, and to assure good substitute parental care in the event of the absence, temporary or permanent inability or unfitness of parents to provide care and protection for their children.

They have to go someplace, the children you read about in the paper, the injured ones with burns and broken arms, the little ones found alone in cold apartments, the frightened ones on the scene when their parents are arrested on drug charges, the glassy-eyed teenagers sleeping on park benches. Sometimes, when beds are scarce, someplace is a hospital or a shelter or a detention center.

Sometimes, someplace is my house. For me, it begins with a knock on the door and a child standing on the porch. For the child, my porch is just another scene in a very long nightmare. Unbeknownst to the child, or to most other people for that matter, an entire drama has played out behind this scene and beyond the eyes of a largely disinterested public.

A doctor or a neighbor or perhaps a teacher has called the county social service department because he or she fears a child is being abused or neglected. The first call goes to a screener. A screener is responsible for deciding whether a situation is serious enough to warrant intervention. A call about a ten-year-old left home unattended after school will be screened out. A call about a four-year-old with gonorrhea will be screened in. What falls between those two scenarios will depend on the discretion of the screener to decide. A faulty decision in either direction can have devastating effects.

If a call is screened in, an investigator is assigned. Social workers who do investigations are a special breed. They never know what they are going to find when they walk into a house. The work is gut wrenching and occasionally dangerous. Sometimes a situation is critical, and the social worker will remove a child immediately, often accompanied by the police. A family resource worker who is on duty during regular business hours will be notified and will begin the arduous process of locating a foster family with an empty bed. But if this happens at night or on a weekend or holiday and the regular channels for finding foster homes are not available, the investigative social worker will notify the social services hot line. Hot-line workers are in place twenty-four hours a day, seven days a week, with a list of people willing to take children in an emergency.

Being a foster parent on the hot-line list is not for everybody. It means broken sleep and interrupted family celebrations, but it also means an opportunity to do some really important emotional first aid for a kid who has just been through the psychological equivalent of being hit by a bus.

Once an investigator has determined that a child needs placement, the case goes to an assessment worker. This worker has forty-five days to put together a picture of a family. He can talk to doctors, teachers, family, and friends. Rules of confidentiality don't apply when a child is at risk. Next, the worker will figure out what the family might need to make it safe for a child to return home. Very often, there will already be a lot of information on file. It is an unfortunate fact that today's abusive parents were yesterday's abused children, and they may very well have a long history with social services.

After the forty-five-day assessment period is over, an ongoing social worker is assigned. This worker is responsible for setting up visitation between children and their families; assisting families in obtaining mental health, housing, and other services; monitoring the care the children receive in their foster homes; attending court hearings; and consulting with psychologists and special education teams. Theoretically, this worker will stay with the child until the family is reunified or the case moves to adoption. Realistically, this rarely happens. The turnover rate for social workers is high. Cases are reassigned on a regular basis, and each new worker has to start all over with a family. Management policy changes with the political and social tides.

Figuring out what to do with an at-risk child is a cumbersome process with a multilevel management system that operates on local, regional, and state levels. The oversight provided by the system is supposed to protect children, and to a certain extent it does. But it also can turn them into faceless, nameless numbers, and foster homes into little more than a bunch of empty beds. This was essentially the way the Department of Social Services (DSS) operated when Bruce and I became foster parents thirteen years ago and the way it continues to operate today.

This flowchart of job descriptions was the sort of basic information that I learned from the thirty hours of training I received from social services before I became a foster parent. It helped, I guess, in the way that it always helps to know how any system you have to work within operates, but in terms of caring for children and figuring out how to make a complicated family function at something above a level of total chaos, the training program was useless. Everything that really mattered I learned from other foster parents and from my own mistakes. No curriculum ever written can fully capture the experience of caring for an abused child.

Our adoptions of Angie and Neddy were finalized almost three years after their arrival. I resigned from my teaching position and began my life as a full-time foster parent, just as frightened and unsure as the first children who came to us. The first weeks hopscotched into months, and gradually I began to grow into the role.

By the time a year had gone by I had managed to acquire most of the trappings of the job. We traded in our car for a van and bought a membership in a warehouse shopping club. I picked up some sage advice at a monthly foster parent support group meeting. I learned that you could never have too many potatoes, towels, or Legos on hand but that it was silly to go overboard on frilly dresses. Some of the best advice I got came from another mother of nine: "In our house," she said, "if they're both socks, they're a pair." That kind of common sense was what the training program forgot to mention.

My friends now settled into two distinct categories. Bruce and I continued to go out to dinner and vacation with the same couples with whom we had socialized for years, but I developed a second set of foster care friends. Some, like me, had given up other careers to chase the dream of making life better for kids, while others had never done anything else. We were an eclectic group, often with little in common beyond our commitment to our children. Within the group we shared everything from baby furniture to department gossip. Only among this group of friends could Bruce and I share our stories—tales of triumph about the families and kids who made it, and stories about lost children and our own broken hearts. The broken heart was another reality that the training curriculum forgot to address, one of the things we learned about on our own. I know that the first time my heart broke, it wasn't my social worker or my family or my friends from the other part of my life I called. It was other foster parents, the ones who had been there and could really understand.

Although I had cared for other children, I think of that heartbreak as the first time I could legitimately claim the title of foster parent. It is like riding a horse. It isn't the falling off but the climbing back on that earns your spurs.

Bruce and I became a hot-line foster home early in our second year of fostering. It was an unusual weekend that didn't include at least one call from a social worker who needed an emergency placement for a child or two. I was just getting to a place where my stomach didn't lurch when the phone rang in the middle of the night, but I hadn't reached the state of nonchalance that I thought was expected of me. As "seasoned" foster parents, we had finally gotten a telephone hookup installed next to the bed so that I could answer hot-line calls before they woke up the rest of the house.

On the first night it was installed, the phone woke me up at midnight. The voice on the other end of the receiver was annoyingly bright and chipper, oblivious to my groggy state. He needed a place for a baby boy. Could I help?

"A ten-month-old? Sure. Bring him over. I'll leave the light on."

By this time, havoc had become somewhat routine. Bruce slept right through the phone call and all of my hurried preparations, which I managed to make without fully waking up. I pulled out the small crib and set it up in our den, then found a clean sleeper and a few diapers. Last, I made up a bottle and curled up in front of the fire in the living room to wait.

What can I say about waiting for a baby? It is a bit like being in labor. Excitement laced with worry, that sense of not being prepared. The questions are one part of fostering that has never changed for me. What in heaven's name have I gotten myself into? What if I can't do it? Suppose the baby screams all night or gets sick? Suppose I do the wrong thing and make things worse? What if I love him and lose him or, worse, what if I don't?

Fortunately, just about the time I work myself into a complete frenzy, I see the lights of a car in my driveway, and my crazies fade out as rapidly as they come on me.

I have, over the years, forgotten most of the hot-line workers who made these storklike, middle-of-the-night deliveries. They are in and out in minutes, and I seldom see them again. But I do remember Miguel. I remember his hands, large and dark, and how gently he held the little blanket-wrapped bundle that was David. This was one worker who didn't seem to be in a hurry to hand me the kid and get back home to bed. In fact, he seemed loath to release him at all.

I took David from Miguel, sat on the sofa with him, and pulled the grungy blanket back from his face.

I am a crier by nature. Sad movies, patriotic commercials, even Hallmark cards get me going. What I saw made me appreciate the few minutes I had to collect myself while Miguel fished around in his briefcase for what I suspect was imaginary paperwork.

I was a foster parent, so of course I had seen some bruised children before, but never such recent injuries and never on a baby. David's face was discolored from his upper lip to the side of his button nose. Several small, unusual bruises dotted one side of his neck. His left eye was swollen nearly shut. I could picture what happened. Someone held David on the back of his neck and slapped him hard across his tiny face.

When I could finally speak, I asked the usual questions about his birthday and health history. It took several minutes for me to ask what I needed to know.

"Who did this?"

"He's been living in a house with five adults, and nobody knows anything," Miguel told me. "The police were called by neighbors because of the fighting. An officer heard the baby crying and asked to see him. We would probably have taken him without the bruises because everybody in the house was drunk. For sure, somebody in that house did a number on this kid. Probably his dad. The guy's got a vicious temper and a problem with alcohol. But if nobody talks, it'll be hard to make any charges stick. Besides, Dad's still a minor; he just turned seventeen and Mom is only fifteen. My guess is, whoever did this is gonna walk."

Miguel left five minutes later, handing me a list of things I needed to do for David. The first item was to contact David's doctor and get him to call the hospital for a full set of skeletals. These are X rays taken of a child's whole body to determine if he or she has ever had any broken bones. Small children are so resilient, they can break a bone and heal with no one ever knowing they have been injured. But the injuries do leave telltale traces that can be seen on X rays, even years after the fact.

I gave David a bath, sickened by the sight of several other bruises in all shades of blue and green on his small body. He quickly polished off one bottle and part of a second before drifting off to sleep.

Sleep was not that easy for me. I spent the remainder of the night on busywork, sorting socks and cleaning out my pocketbook in a futile effort to wind down and get my mind off thoughts of David's family.

David slept late into the morning, so I had a chance to prepare Bruce and the children for his face. Even so, they were silent when I picked him up and they got their first look. It was especially hard on Angie, who had been battered herself.

As soon as I expected his office to open, I called David's doctor. I left a message with his receptionist, and within minutes Dr. Dupont called me back.

"I'll schedule the X rays, but the whole thing is nonsense, in my opinion. Social services had no business pulling that child from a two-parent family to put him in some foster home. Even if one of them did lose his temper and give him a swat or two, it's hardly the end of the world. He'll probably suffer far more from missing his mother than he will from a little overzealous discipline."

I looked at David, sitting in the high chair, happily chomping his way through Cheerios and sliced bananas. His eye had turned a darker purple overnight. He caught my eye and gave me a big toothy grin, in spite of the swollen lip. He was a sweet little thing. Soft apricot curls framed what should have been a perfect Gerber face. There was no point in arguing with Dr. Dupont. "When should I bring him in?" I asked.

"You can bring him to the E.R. now, but you'll probably have to wait a while. They have sick people to see."

I hung up feeling defensive and a bit put upon. I only received fifteen dollars a day for taking a child for hot line. Out of that, I paid for diapers, formula, baby wipes, and all of the extras that babies need. Now I would also pay for child care for the morning. I didn't mind losing money, but I sure minded being insulted, and I really minded the cavalier way that David's doctor took my report of his injuries. It was clear he was no fan of foster care in general or me in particular. I was already pretty ragged from no sleep, and that unpleasant conversation was the last thing I needed.

It took nearly an hour to get the older kids off to school, find a baby-sitter, and get out the door, leaving behind a sink full of dirty dishes and more laundry than I cared to think about, along with a couple of children crying and unhappy about not coming with me.

Waiting for the X rays was really embarrassing. People looked at David, did a double take, and then glared at me. In truth, he looked awful, and they had no way of knowing I wasn't responsible. At one time, I might have had the same reaction.

It was a relief to have the X-ray technician come to take David from me but a short-lived one. David's radar was, out of necessity, better developed than that in most children, and this stranger in the white coat taking him from me did not go over well. David let out a wail and struggled to get back to me. If anyone had missed us before, they saw us now. I think there were a couple of folks ready to jump out of their wheelchairs and leap to David's defense if I should make any move to hit him. Not for the last time, I wished for a T-shirt that said "Don't blame me. I'm just the foster mom."

In a mercifully short period of time, the X rays were completed and we were headed home.

My sitter, Dawn, was waiting for me with a fistful of phone messages. The ones from Tanya's attorney and Danny's social worker could wait, but I wanted to return Dr. Dupont's right away.

Dr. Dupont stammered and stumbled before he got to the point.

"I think I might owe you a bit of an apology," he began. "It had been a long night, and I was, perhaps, a bit gruff. Anyway, the hospital just called me with the results of David's X rays." The doctor hesitated a moment. "He's had five broken ribs, and his arm has healed fractures. This has apparently been going on for months. Most of the breaks are well healed. I haven't seen David often, but still this is a shock to me. His parents are young but . . ."

The sentence drifted off. There really wasn't much to say.

"Have you filed the abuse report yet?"

"Yes. The hospital has too. I'm sure you'll be hearing from someone. Will David be staying with you?"

"I don't know. I already have one more kid than I'm supposed to, but we'll keep him if we can."

"Well, thank you for taking him. Please let me know if he's moved. I'd like to keep seeing him if possible."

I got the other kids occupied with crayons and paper and made David a fresh bottle.

There was so much I couldn't do. I couldn't erase the last ten months for David. I couldn't make any promises for the future. For now, I could keep him safe and warm. I could rock him and sing him a lullaby, which is what I did until he fell asleep in my arms.

At that moment, foster care became not just something I did but part of who I was and who I could be. I could make a difference, a real difference in a child's life. This baby would never know about me. Still, because I had loved him, cared about him, I was a part of him. It made me feel that what I did mattered in a way it hadn't before.

The ambivalence that troubled me from my earliest days with social services vanished. That isn't to say that I always felt social services did the right thing. Mistakes, catastrophic mistakes, were sometimes made. In spite of that, I believed that all of us tried to do our best to make life better for these children. I felt like one of the good guys.

David stayed with us for only a week. His young mother, Amber, was pregnant again, to everyone's dismay. Social services offered her a deal. She could go into foster care with David. She would get services until she was ready to be independent. The only stipulation was that she stay away from David's father, Tony. She agreed, and by Monday she and David had moved in with the Millers, one of the two local families who took pregnant and parenting teens.

I exercised what was for me admirable if not downright amazing restraint and didn't call to check on David until he'd had plenty of time to settle into his new situation. Three weeks after he left my home, I had Pam Miller on the phone. "David's not here anymore," she told me.

"What do you mean?" I said. "Where is he?"

"His mom changed her mind about accepting services," Pam answered. "She's back with Tony. I only do parenting for pregnant teens so I couldn't keep David. He was moved to Lydia's last week. I meant to call you, but you know how it is."

I hung up feeling depressed. David needed to settle someplace. Bouncing around like this was terrible for him. If he didn't have permanence soon, he would be at risk for all kinds of attachment problems. I wished I had room to keep him.

I tried to keep track of David, but it wasn't easy. I had met Lydia, his new foster mother, only once, and I didn't feel like I should call too often.

Pam Miller called me six weeks after David had moved to Lydia's. She had run into Lydia at a training seminar and gotten an update on David. The case had gone to court, and to everybody's surprise, the judge had ruled that David be placed with Tony's sister, who had claimed ignorance of David's injuries when he was first removed from his parents' custody. I knew the case would remain open and that social services would be keeping a very close eye on the baby, as would his doctor, but I still felt that David wasn't safe and that the judge had betrayed him by choosing his family over foster care because of the perception that any family, however bad, was inherently better than any foster home, however good. It was tough to be too critical for long, though, because in the past I had sometimes felt the same way.

I heard about David's family one final time. Pam Miller called me one bright May morning. She sounded odd, not her usual chatty self.

"Have you seen the paper today?"

I hadn't, of course. I rarely had time to read it before the evening.

"Read it and call me back," Pam said. "I can't talk right now."

The details were a bit sketchy, but I knew enough about the family to fill in some of the blanks. After losing custody of David, Tony and a very pregnant Amber moved to New Hampshire to start over. There was no process for tracking them from state to state, and besides, Tony was never accused, much less convicted, of a crime.

In April, Amber gave birth to a baby, another son she named Joshua. Sometime in the early hours of a spring morning, Tony lost his temper again. This time he beat his infant son to death.

That was very nearly the end of foster care for me. Joshua's death exemplified everything wrong with the social service system. This was a baby who should not have died. But then I thought about David. Somewhere, deep inside him, was the memory of being safe and cared for, however briefly. Maybe it would make a difference someday. That's what helped me hang on through the hard days and the sleepless nights. I had a chance to make a difference.

There was no way for me to look into the future and see exactly what I was getting into. If I could have foreseen children like Danny or Sara in my life, maybe I would have run for the hills. But I didn't know and I didn't run. On the contrary. I jumped in with both feet, mercifully unaware of all that the coming years would bring.

Chapter

Two

❖

Bruce and I continued doing hot-line work, but we were also taking children for longer placements. The biggest need in our area was for families willing to provide homes for teenagers. With five adolescents of our own, that was not something I wanted to tackle. The other population that was difficult to place was infants. Babies are often perceived as a lot more trouble than they're "worth." In addition to per diem reimbursement, foster parents receive an additional fifty dollars every three months for clothing. WIC, the nutritional support program for women, infants, and children under five, will give vouchers for formula, but everything else, from diapers to child care, comes out of the pocket of the foster parent. And there is a lot of everything else, things like baby wipes and crib sheets and car seats. Babies require extra time as well. They have more doctors' appointments than older kids and often more visitation with birth families. Middle-of-the-night feedings, teething, and colic are not for everyone.

That makes it a little hard to explain why I so much wanted one. Goodness knows, my hands were already very full. Our five children were growing up. Bruce Jr. was eighteen; Nate, sixteen; and Ben, nearly fourteen. Angie and Neddy had grown into lovely young ladies of ten and twelve. Now that I had a couple of years of experience under my belt, I had started taking tougher kids, kids with serious behavior problems and developmental delays. I guess that with so many children coming to me with such huge problems, I needed the innocence and relatively clean slate of a baby to give myself some perspective. I loved the feeling of having another chance to get it right for a child. But it had been several months since we had had a baby for more than a day or two, and I was getting itchy. Which may explain then, why, when a social worker called and asked if I would be willing to drive to the courthouse in the next town and pick up a seven-month-old girl named Karen, I was in my van and on the road in under an hour.

A photograph taken in my house the day Karen arrived shows a rather motley little bunch of children, all of whom look surprisingly unremarkable, considering what they had been through. Danny was eight and had been with us the longest, well over a year. Poor Danny was a Murphy's Law kind of kid. Whatever could have gone wrong for him in eight short years had done so. His mother was the product of deinstitutionalization. When the Massachusetts State psychiatric hospitals began emptying their beds in the 1980s because of the deplorable conditions in most facilities, people who needed a fairly sophisticated level of care were often discharged to the street. Many with diagnoses of retardation, schizophrenia, or psychosis soon had the added problem of drug addiction to contend with. This was Dan's mother. It was never clear exactly why someone as disabled as she was ever allowed to take a baby home from the hospital, but she was, and it was a disaster from the beginning.

All babies have pretty basic needs. They get hungry and cold and tired and bored. They let the world know they need something by crying. In most cases, a parent picks up her fussing infant and tries out one thing, then another, until the baby's need is met and he or she settles down again. The baby feels good; the parent feels good. This cycle happens over and over, day after day. Most parents don't give it much thought. It's instinctive. It's the way babies attach to parents and parents to babies.

For Danny, the cycle never got started. How could it? Pearl could barely meet her own needs, much less Danny's. He got hungry and cried all night. Sometimes he even got a bottle. But the bottle might have soured milk in it, or it might have Kool-Aid. He might get cuddled or he might get smacked. Sometimes he got screamed at, and sometimes he was left alone in a darkened room to cry for hours. By the time Danny was a year old, he had figured out that the world was a pretty unpredictable place and not much fun. He no longer cried. He stopped trying to please people. By the time he was three he learned to take what he wanted and to hurt people before he could be hurt.

It doesn't take much imagination to picture the kind of man who would be attracted to his mother. When Danny was lucky, Pearl's boyfriends just ignored him. When he was not so lucky, they saw Pearl's frail, underweight, silent boy as the perfect victim. He never fought back, and there was no one he could tell about the abuse.

Danny was finally rescued by an observant Head Start teacher who refused to accept Pearl's excuses for Danny's burns and bruises and split lips. She called social services, and, at four, Danny began a rocky journey into the foster care system. Danny's main problem, through no fault of his own, was that he had managed to become invisible to all of the people who should have been helping him. He was retarded, but the Department of Mental Retardation wouldn't provide services because he was mentally ill. The Department of Mental Health wouldn't provide services because he was retarded. He was always somebody else's problem. DSS was stuck with him but they had no plan for him. He was the kind of child they do the worst by. He could certainly never go home again, but he wasn't seen as a candidate for adoption.

Even a foster home was hard to come by. By the time he came to us, Danny had already bounced through a couple of homes and acquired a reputation as a very tough placement. He could be dangerous, unpredictable, and, scariest of all, he showed all the signs of being a budding pedophile. We quickly learned to never, ever leave Danny alone with a younger child.

We had some small successes though. Danny was nearly toilet trained now, although he still wet the bed every night. He had put on some much-needed weight and seemed much more physically coordinated once we got him glasses that fit. Still, Danny was a hard kid to love, a hard kid to help.

Sitting next to Danny in the picture was two-year-old Tyler, who was as different from Danny as a child could be. Where Danny was homely, with protruding ears, thick glasses, and buck-teeth, Tyler was adorable. With a head full of blond curls, wide chocolate-brown eyes, and deep dimples, he looked like a kid on a Christmas card. His beauty was marred only by the presence of a large purple lump smack in the middle of his forehead—the visible result of Tyler's tantrums. Several times a day something would set him off. What began with a sirenlike screaming usually ended with Tyler banging his head over and over on the hardest surface he could find. No one knew what was really going on with Ty. Was he so difficult because he was abused, or did his mother abuse him because he was so difficult?

When Ty played with our dollhouse, that miniature master-piece of Victorian splendor became a place you would never want to live. The babies would be routinely flushed down the toilets or locked in closets. Daddy dolls threw Mama dolls down stairs, and Mama dolls screamed and knocked over furniture. It was a pretty scary world that Ty inhabited.

Still, between tantrums, he was a sweet little guy and, after six months, was beginning to look a bit better. He continued to have violent episodes, but they were getting shorter and less intense. His parents were doing all the right things: They visited regularly and met with the social worker every week. The plan was for Tyler to return home in time for Christmas. But there was an edginess about them that made me nervous, as though they were on their best behavior around me but just holding on by a thread. And Lila, Tyler's mom, was obviously and unexpectedly pregnant. It was a fragile, unhappy little family, and, while I wished them well, it was hard to be optimistic for them.

The next child in the photo was Lucy. She was eight, a dear little girl with a face as long and thin and plain as a platter. Lucy had no organic problems and hadn't suffered the same kind of flagrant abuse that marked Danny and Ty. Rather, Lucy had been consistently ignored. Her mother, Ellen, had been only fifteen when she found herself pregnant with Lucy. At first, she was charmed by her infant, then annoyed, and finally indifferent. She dragged Lucy along in her escapades like a bedraggled rag doll. Lucy attended school only sporadically and was always behind on her shots. As an infant, she was hospitalized twice for dehydration and failure-to-thrive syndrome.

Social services did not remove Lucy from her home, which isn't surprising, because it's very hard to make a case in court for removal because of neglect. Judges prefer the more obvious signs of abuse. Rather, Ellen had dumped her child, claiming that she was "fried" with the constant care Lucy required and that she needed a break. A break from what was my question. Ellen didn't cook or clean or do more than essential laundry. Lucy didn't even have a bed. She slept on the sofa each night and either got herself off to school or chose to stay home. I worked hard to like Ellen, but she didn't make it easy. She rarely visited and seldom called. Foster care seemed to make it easy for her to continue to neglect her child.

Lucy was not a talkative kid and by nature quite solemn. Connecting with us was hard for her as she had had little experience with adults she could count on. But she liked Angie and Neddy, and they were great about including her in whatever they were doing. She and Bruce enjoyed each other's company too. Lucy was a tomboy and glad to help with yard work and house projects.

Slowly, Lucy's personality began to emerge. She could be quite funny and very kind. She wasn't a great or even good student, but she always tried hard. She was the kind of kid who was easy to have around, and Lord knows, I needed an easy one with Danny and Tyler to deal with.

The day Karen came, I snapped several pictures. All of my children came from chaotic backgrounds, and none of them had seen many pictures of themselves, cameras and films being luxury items. They all took great delight in photographic evidence that they were noticed and cared for.

When these family pictures were developed, Lucy looked at them for a long time, long after the others had lost interest. She ran her finger over each image. "Well," she said finally, "a picture of fosters. I think I know what happened. First my mom was with Earl, but he went to jail; so they broke up. Then she was with Bob, but his wife got real mad; so then they broke up. Then she was with Digger, but he hit her all the time and they broke up. Now I guess my mom broke up with me, but I don't know what I did."

Lucy's eyes filled up but she wouldn't cry. I wondered if she knew how.

On the early spring day that I arrived at the courthouse to pick up Karen, I met an officer at the court door and, after being checked for concealed weapons, was led into a room not much larger than a coat closet and dominated by a large table. It was a strange scene. A couple sat on the floor in one corner with a handsome little boy of perhaps four or five between them. Two women sat in another corner, cuddling a baby who looked younger than the seven-month-old I was here to pick up. One of the women was crying softly, and the other was trying to comfort her. A middle-aged man sat at the end of the table. He could only have been a lawyer, with his distinguished white hair, three-piece suit, power tie, and briefcase.

When I entered, everyone looked up. There were a couple of tentative smiles but no one spoke. I couldn't very well just take the baby and walk out; this was just the kind of awkward moment that was never addressed in our training program.

The tension finally got the better of me.

"I'm Mrs. Harrison," I said to no one in particular. "This must be Karen."

The attorney looked up and smiled.

"I figured that might be who you were. I'm Sam Zdiarski, the child's attorney. Sam is fine. Most people have trouble with my last name. And, yes, this little beauty is Karen."

The door opened and three more people entered the room: another lawyer type; a social worker, Linda, who I recognized from the DSS office; and a young woman who could only be Karen's mother. The nose ring and short spiked hair didn't disguise her delicate beauty.

She went over to the little boy, knelt to kiss him, and left the room quickly. She didn't look at Karen.

Her attorney followed her out the door, but Linda stayed behind to do the introductions and help me carry Karen and her things out to my car. "That was Bonnie Kincaid, Karen's mother," Linda said. "I suppose you guessed. This is Ryan, Karen's big brother. And this is his aunt and uncle. Ryan will be staying with them, so you might want to talk to them about visitation. It's important for Karen and Ryan to see each other."

Linda walked over to the baby and the two women holding

her. One of them, Deb, fumbled through her purse for a piece of paper. It was a detailed account of Karen's history: her schedule, her likes, her dislikes, and a list of all the people in her life. There were numbers for everyone and the dates of upcoming appointments. It must have taken hours to put together, and I was more grateful than I could say.

"We'd like to keep her," Deb said. "We really would, but our apartment is so small and we both work full-time. She'd be in day care all the time."

It was plain that Karen was being well cared for. She was clean and nicely dressed. More important, she was snuggled next to Deb in a comfortable, natural way, her tiny hand reaching up to touch Deb's cheek. When Deb looked down and smiled, Karen broke into an ear-to-ear grin. She was a pretty baby, with huge blue eyes and rosy cheeks. Her hair was so white as to be nearly invisible. When I put my hands out to pick her up, Deb winced. I had, in the past, been put in the position of handing over a baby I would have just as soon kept, so I could guess how Deb was feeling. I made my getaway as quickly as possible.

Karen fell asleep on the way home and remained asleep when I brought her inside. I was glad for the quiet time. Tyler was due back from a visit with his family at two, and the other kids would be home soon. I wanted to look over Karen's history and figure out how I was going to fit in taking her to visit Bonnie a half day each week. Bonnie's mother had died when Bonnie was little, and she was raised by an alcoholic stepmother and a chronically depressed father. Two older sisters had problems with substance abuse. By the time she was fifteen, Bonnie was drinking heavily too. She was pregnant with Ryan at fifteen and pregnant again eighteen months later. This child, a girl, was with her father. At nineteen she was pregnant with Karen. She managed to stay away from drugs and alcohol during her first two pregnancies but slipped shortly thereafter. She wanted to do better with Karen, so she checked into a program for pregnant and parenting women who were battling drug and alcohol abuse.

The program was the first family Bonnie ever really had. They gave her a lot of support throughout the pregnancy and helped her get set up in an apartment. Once she was settled in her new home with Ryan and Karen, a mental health clinician saw her twice a week, and a visiting nurse checked in often as well. The program provided transportation and child care so that Bonnie could attend AA meetings and a support group.

Even so, things didn't go well. Without the structure of living in the center, Bonnie quickly fell apart. Within a week, she was depressed and suicidal. Karen was always sick, and Ryan got cranky and oppositional from being inside too much.

Bonnie's counselor was very concerned and suggested Bonnie check into the psychiatric unit of a hospital affiliated with the substance abuse program. Ryan went to his aunt's; Karen stayed with Deb for a week and then came to me. Bonnie got out of the hospital on a day pass to attend the court hearing when DSS assumed legal custody of both children.

The plan was pretty straightforward: Bonnie would be in the hospital for another week. When released, she would return to her apartment. The children would each visit for a half day, once a week. After a month, they would spend a full day together with her, then a weekend, then move back for good with a provision for some respite child care if Bonnie appeared to be getting overwhelmed.

According to Deb's notes, Karen was hard to deal with. She had a chronic ear infection that wasn't responding to medication, so she was in pain a lot and always seemed to have a fever. She cried a good deal and was hard to soothe. It didn't take long for me to see what she meant: Karen was a challenge. Each night, after her bath, I laid her in front of the fireplace, and, in the soft glow, I rubbed her arms and legs with lotion. The massage seemed to soothe her enough so that I could get her to sleep, although she awoke crying several times at night. Many nights I slept in the recliner with the baby tucked in my arms. Those nights were long, but I never resented the hours I spent with Karen.

When she wasn't sick, Karen was a joy. She smiled and cooed and giggled out loud. Bruce picked her up as soon as he walked in the door and seldom put her down until bedtime. That allowed me some uninterrupted time to help Danny and Lucy with their schoolwork and to read to Tyler.

Karen's first visit with Bonnie was tense. Bonnie's apartment was immaculate, and she was good with Karen, loving and affectionate, but very defensive with me. I understood. It must feel awful to have a stranger come into your home and tell you how to raise your own child. I knew it was important for me to connect with Bonnie if I was going to help her figure out how to parent Karen, so I kept my interference to a bare minimum. But one thing I couldn't ignore was the cigarette smoke. Bonnie always seemed to be lighting up. Because of Karen's health problems I was a bit of a fanatic about her environment. No one was allowed to smoke in our house anyway, and I wouldn't take Karen anyplace where I thought someone might smoke. When I suggested that the smoke might not be good for the baby, Bonnie bristled, but she did put her cigarette out.

I was glad when the visit was over and I could get Karen home. For some reason, I felt odd watching Bonnie care for her. I wanted to jump in and show Bonnie how I changed Karen's diapers and fixed her lunch. My stomach did a funny little lurch when Bonnie rocked her baby. It was hard to give the feeling a name. If pressed, I might have been forced to admit I was jealous.

The second visit was even harder. Karen had had a tough couple of days. She had started wheezing and developed croup. I, of course, was quick to blame the previous week's exposure to cigarette smoke. I had spent three nights following that visit in a steamy bathroom with a baby who struggled for each breath. Karen stayed clingy for the rest of the week.

We got to Bonnie's a few minutes early. I took a squirming Karen out of her snowsuit and handed her to her mother. A lit cigarette lay in an ashtray on the table. I mentioned the croup and suggested that smoke might aggravate Karen's cough.

"She's been croupy since she was born. I don't think it's the smoke," Bonnie snapped. "I think I know what's best for my own daughter. You're not her mother." No, I thought. I'm not. I'm just the lady who will sit up all night worrying about her when she can't breathe. Bonnie's attitude brought out the worst in me. It probably didn't help that she wasn't a great deal older than my oldest son. I really had to fight the urge to tell her to watch her manners and do as I said.

That day, I was supposed to go shopping and let Bonnie cope with Karen for a few hours. Just before I left, a friend of Bonnie's stopped by with a coughing toddler and a lit cigarette. She was still there when I came back to retrieve Karen a couple of hours later. Karen was sleeping in the playpen, and the woman's little boy was parked in front of the television. Bonnie and her friend were chatting away over coffee. I had hoped to find that Bonnie had spent her visitation time with Karen focused entirely on her baby's needs, but that didn't seem to be the case. I knew that Karen hadn't had a diaper change (I counted the diapers), and my guess was that she spent the morning in that playpen. My hands shook when I got her dressed, and I barely said good-bye. That kind of thing still happens to me a lot, but I don't stew about it quite like I stewed about Bonnie and Karen.

At the time, I was still learning an important lesson for foster parents: There are lots of ways to take care of children, and they aren't all going to be the way I would do it. That doesn't necessarily make my way right and someone else's wrong. Knowing what I know now makes me a lot less critical about overdue diaper changes or hours spent in the confines of a playpen. Diapers are expensive, and sometimes a playpen is the only safe place in an apartment.

This visit was followed by another tough week. Karen was coughing and wheezing again before we got home. We spent the next two nights in the bathroom, and Karen ended up on another round of antibiotics.

The next Sunday afternoon I called Bonnie to confirm our Monday morning visit. She sounded even more annoyed than usual when I called. She snapped when I asked her if everything was all right.

"Of course I'm all right. And you'll need to dress Karen in

something nice. I'm having her picture taken. Put her in something Christmassy."

I resisted the urge to slam down the phone and another urge to lay out some overalls for the following day. Instead, I got out the holiday dress I had just bought for Karen and made a note to myself to call Karen's social worker and her attorney and ask them to confront the issue of Bonnie's smoking.

I drove to Bonnie's through an icy, gray drizzle. The wind was picking up and the roads were slick. Twice, I considered returning home to my fireplace, some hot tea, and a good murder mystery, but both times I decided to trudge on. The weather was supposed to improve by midmorning, and I didn't want to make the visit up. Mondays were the only weekday Tyler spent with his mother. On any other day, I would need to find child care, and few baby-sitters were willing to put up with the tantrums he still had when I left him.

Bonnie's house looked forbidding. It was actually an attractive duplex in a decent neighborhood, but today every shade was pulled down and there was an unfamiliar car in the parking area.

I woke Karen, wrestled her from her car seat, and approached the door. Bonnie was usually waiting to open it since I was struggling with a purse, diaper bag, and a snow-suited baby, but on this morning the door remained closed. I knocked several times. Muted adult voices could be heard inside but no one responded. I could hear another, softer voice as well, but the words were indistinguishable. I thought the voices came from a television or radio. I knocked a few more times and rattled the doorknob, but still no one came to the door.

The wind was really howling. After several minutes, I gave up and returned to my car. The only idea that occurred to me was to go to the 7-Eleven on the corner and call Bonnie's house from a pay phone. Maybe Bonnie was in the shower or vacuuming. Perhaps she was drying her hair. Of course, I had no coins for the phone. This meant dragging Karen out of her car seat again so that I could go get some. I struggled to hold the baby in one arm, fumbling with the quarter and the phone with the other hand. A prerecorded out-of-service message answered on the first ring.

I tried again and got the same response. I piled a very unhappy Karen back into the car seat and returned to Bonnie's. Surely by now she would answer the door.

I knocked again. Something about the whole situation felt very wrong.

I went back to the 7-Eleven, searched for another quarter, and thumbed through my address book for the number of the social services office, aware of Karen's screams from the car as I tried to reach Linda.

Linda, of course, wasn't there, so I spoke to the duty day worker. She heard the story but was less concerned than I.

"Try the door once more. If you don't get a response, call 911. It's still possible that she's in the shower or something. There's no point in overreacting."

Once again, I returned to Bonnie's. Karen seemed to have gained several pounds since I left home with her that morning. I left the diaper bag in the car, pulled the baby out of the car seat, and approached the door.

I knocked really loudly. Still no one answered, but this time I definitely heard a voice inside. I rattled the doorknob. The door was a cheap, hollow-core model. I gave it a solid kick, and the flimsy lock gave way. The door eerily swung open into Bonnie's darkened living room. The only light came from the television set in the corner, which was tuned to a frantic game show. A stout little grandmother was showering a grinning host with kisses, delirious over her new washer/dryer combo.

It took a moment for my eyes to adjust to the low level of light, and when they did, I saw the body right away. It looked as though she had fallen asleep sitting up and then slumped to one side. At least it wasn't Bonnie. This girl had long, dark hair.

I took a deep breath and steeled myself to touch her wrist. I'm not brave and it wasn't easy, especially with Karen on my hip. The hand felt cold and was a dusky blue. I couldn't find a pulse, but it was hard to tell over my own heart pounding. I had to walk around the body to reach the phone, not remembering until I picked it up and heard only silence that it was disconnected.

I took another deep breath to settle my stomach and organize my thoughts.

This poor woman, hardly more than a child really, was dead. Bonnie was probably here somewhere. I considered going to look for her when I was startled by a small sound. In the dark, I could make out the figure of a tiny child wedged between the wall and the sofa. Even with the low level of light, I recognized him. It was the little boy with the cold from last week. That was his mother lying on the sofa. Until that moment, I hadn't focused on the clutter on the coffee table. Needles, pills, and small vials of who knew what littered the surface.

The child whimpered and tried to back further into the corner. He held a filthy teddy bear in his arms.

"Come on, sweetie, can you come see me? I'll bet you're hungry. I'll get you something to eat."

"Mommy up. Tell mommy up." His little voice was choked with tears.

He was hardly more than a baby, probably not quite two. I hated to be rough, but I had two babies, a room full of drugs, and at least one dead body. He couldn't stay here, and I needed to get to a phone.

I took his arm and pulled him out. He was soaking wet in his pajamas, and it was freezing outside. Trying to keep myself between him and his mother, I slipped out of my coat, wrapped it around his tiny body, then hoisted Karen on one hip and the boy on the other and went to my car.

Karen rebelled once again at being forced into her car seat. Her body was stiff with rage. After several minutes, I got her strapped in her seat. I made every attempt to get a seat belt around the little boy, but he was hysterical, clawing my face and screaming for his mother.

"Come on, God," I whispered. "A little help here."

A tiny blue car pulled to the shoulder, blinker on, preparing to pull into the parking lot. I recognized the driver.

Hallelujah! It was Deb from the courthouse, here for a visit. I have had prayers answered before but never quite so quickly.

I began rattling off my somewhat incoherent story before Deb was fully out of her car. Before I finished, she was already running to the house. She emerged in seconds.

"Rhonda is dead. Bonnie's still with us but she needs an ambulance. There's got to be someone home around here. I'll go find a phone. You move the cars so they can get in."

I was happy to follow orders. My brain seemed to have stopped working anyway.

The next several hours sped by. An officer appeared and offered to drive my car to the police station so I could give a statement and file a report with social services. He wanted to call Bruce for me but I wouldn't let him. I was fine, I insisted. I just wanted a quiet place to feed and change Karen and a cup of tea. There was no reason to call Bruce. What could he do? I was fine. Really!

Brian, a DSS worker, showed up to sit with me, and someone else came to get the little boy. I wrote out reports, spoke to detectives, spoke to social workers, was told not to speak to the press, and drank cup after cup of lukewarm, vending machine tea.

There was one amusing moment. I asked a young police officer if I might use the microwave I could clearly see in the officers' lounge to heat up Karen's bottle. He refused. It was not for civilian use. "Come on," I insisted. "She's not a civilian. She's eight months old and she prefers a warm bottle. It'll take thirty seconds." My pleas were lost on him. No way. I wasn't allowed in there.

Something snapped. I'm not usually confrontational, but I had really had it. I said something about Nazis and something else about the press.

"Now I have not had a good day," I finished. "I want a warm bottle and I want it now." I heard a faint chuckle behind me from a gentleman with lots of stripes and little metal pins.

"Under the circumstances, I think we might make an exception," he said with a smile.

It was a small and short-lived victory. When I was finally allowed to go home, I found my car with a bright yellow ticket under the wiper.

I managed to hold myself together until I had seen the children home from school, supervised some homework, and gotten supper started. I didn't, in fact, fall apart until Bruce walked in the door. That was it. I completely broke down, crying and shaking as I told him the whole awful story.

He was angry and maybe a little hurt that I hadn't called him to sit with me at the police station, but I honestly hadn't realized how much I needed his firm, steady support until I was in his arms. He was worried too. When we had signed up to be foster parents it had not occurred to either one of us that dead bodies would be part of the deal.

That evening, after fielding a dozen phone calls, I got Karen bathed and powdered and tucked her into her fuzzy pink sleepers. I packed away her Christmas dress. I rocked her quietly in front of the fire, watching her face relax into sleep. I kept seeing the terrified eyes of the little boy, crouched in the corner while his mother lay dead on the sofa. I whispered a prayer and a promise, my mantra, my mission: You are safe. I will keep you safe. You will always be safe. I admitted what I had known from the minute I held her. I cared about all the children who came to us, battered and bruised. Some, I even allowed myself to love. But Karen was different. Karen was mine.

Chapter

Three

My recovery from the shock of finding a body in Bonnie's living room was sped along by the approaching holidays. Bonnie entered another rehabilitation program, and visitation for Karen was suspended, at least for the moment. Other than her health problems, Karen was a delight. She was a cuddler and a smiler. The entire household was smitten with her. She was particularly good for Danny. He had never had the kind of love Karen offered, without reservation and without expectations. She didn't care if he couldn't count much past ten or tie his shoes or stay dry. Her face lit up every time he entered the room, and he was at his most animated with her. Tyler was less impressed. He was so needy that the competition was hard for him. He was making only fair progress, and I often wished I could have offered him a family with fewer children and more time.

Christmas morning erupted in an amazing avalanche of paper,

bows, and noise that only large families can fully appreciate. Neither Danny nor Tyler had ever experienced anything quite like it,
and both reacted with predictable unpredictability. Danny slipped
off, ostensibly to get his robe, but ended up in the bathroom trying to devour a gingerbread ornament. The fact that it was made
of wax didn't seem to deter him. Tyler refused to open anything
until after an impressive tantrum. Lucy was her usual quiet self. I
suspected that her pleasure over her large pile of gifts was tem-
pered by her mother's failure to call as promised. Karen ignored
her presents and spent the morning climbing through the clutter
and munching on ribbons.

By ten o'clock, things began to wind down. Bruce started to
pick up wrapping paper, and the older kids ferried gifts to their
owners' bedrooms while I bathed the little ones and supervised
Danny's shower. I thought I heard the phone ring and was glad to
have Karen's bath provide me with a legitimate excuse for ignoring
it. I was happily watching Karen splash in the tub when Angie
joined me in the bathroom.

"I'll get Karen dressed, Mom," she said. "You might want to go
into the living room and kill Daddy."

"Any particular reason?"

"Hot line just called, and he told them we'd take a baby.
They're on their way."

I didn't kill Bruce, but I did question his sanity. We could have
coped for a day or two, but these were not normal circumstances.
I had a very full house, and, with the extended school holiday, the
chances of a baby being moved out any time soon were not good.

The baby, whom we called Gracie, had been found, abandoned, on the doorstep of a church. At first, the aging sexton

thought the basket sitting on the steps contained food for the shelter program the church helped support. When he saw the tiny girl inside, he immediately called the police. Within minutes, every television station and newspaper in the area had picked up the story. There was nothing quite like it for tugging at heartstrings and grabbing headlines. The department needed someplace quiet and out of the way to stash this baby while they searched for her family. While less remote than the farm, our house was still out in the country and just what they were looking for.

Gracie was delivered just in time to assure that I would not have time to eat my dinner, but one look at her perfect little face was enough to put all thoughts of turkey out of my mind. She was, quite simply, the most exquisite baby I had ever seen. She looked to be not much over a month old, with lovely blue eyes and a head of dark hair. Had I been looking for a Christmas angel, Gracie would have fit the bill.

Keeping this baby a secret was not going to be easy. She was big news, and people did drop in from time to time. It wouldn't take a brain surgeon to put two and two together and figure out that Gracie and Baby Jane Doe were one and the same. But the police and social services were adamant. There were to be no breaches in confidentiality on this case. After the officials left, I sat the children down and explained the situation to them. They nodded solemnly and swore themselves to secrecy, but I wasn't fooled for an instant. They were only kids, and they all loved being the center of attention. I gave it one week, two at the most, before one of them spilled the beans.

I worried about taking Gracie out in public, but sometimes it just couldn't be avoided. On her third day with us, I took her for a checkup with our local pediatrician and stopped at a local thrift shop to pick up some clothes for her on the way home. The police had kept everything Gracie was wearing when she was abandoned, but it wasn't much and I had very little that was small enough for her.

A lovely Irish lady waited on me. She offered to hold Gracie and said while I wrote out a check, "Isn't she just the sweetest little thing? It's so nice to see one who is getting the proper care and attention. When I think about that poor little mite, dropped off like a sack of potatoes, why it makes my blood boil." The "poor little mite" smiled up at her. "I expect the wee girl is in one of those awful foster places you hear about. Heaven knows what will happen to her." She handed me my purchases with a smile. "Now you take good care of this baby. She's a lucky little girl, she is." I didn't worry so much about people recognizing Gracie after that. I just didn't mention I was a foster parent when she was with me.

My real problem was time. Bruce and I now had in our home two babies under a year; a disturbed three-year-old; a retarded, disturbed six-year-old; and a very depressed Lucy, in addition to our own five children. Tyler's return to his parents had been delayed for a few weeks, so I couldn't expect even a small respite from the demands until then.

I had a schedule that sometimes worked. I rose at five A.M. with Gracie. She got a change and a bottle and went back to bed until nine. Karen got up at six. I changed her, and Bruce gave her a bottle while he caught the news before work. Tyler got up at seven. I gave him a quick bath and got him dressed, and one of the older kids fixed him breakfast. Danny got up next. I supervised his shower. If I didn't stand right there, he would stand under scalding water until it ran out or pour all the shampoo down the drain. He dressed himself while I fed Karen some cereal. The boys showered in the morning, the girls the night before, and they all fixed breakfast for themselves and cleaned up their own messes. After the school crowd left, I bathed Gracie and fed her again. In between baths and meals, I got Danny's sheets in the wash and tried to grab a bagel. I couldn't get a shower unless all three younger kids napped at the same time.

Nights were easier. The girls helped out with the babies, and the boys kept an eye on Tyler and Danny. Everyone pitched in with dinner and dishes. It would have been fine if Gracie hadn't needed a feeding at eleven P.M. and two A.M., and Karen not been waking for a bottle at three A.M. By the end of the first week I was bleary-eyed, and by the end of the second I was a zombie. I craved a full night of sleep. I even considered requesting that a new home be found for Gracie. There was still no sign of her family, and this was looking more and more like a very long-term placement.

That decision, however, was taken out of my hands just as I anticipated it would be.

The newspapers remained full of Gracie stories, and we continued to caution the children to say nothing if the subject should come up. Even so, it was no surprise when Angie came home one day with a manila envelope filled with articles from the local papers.

"Where did you get these?" I asked her.

"Oh, Mrs. Douglas thought you might like them."

"Now why would Mrs. Douglas think that?"

"Well, because we have the baby."

"How did Mrs. Douglas know we have the baby?"

"I guess I might have told her. I didn't think you'd mind. She's a teacher. She's not going to say anything."

I couldn't be too angry with Angie. It was a pretty hard secret to keep. But I did call Gracie's social worker to let her know that Gracie's whereabouts were no longer confidential. That was at three. At five, a worker arrived to pick her up. They couldn't risk the press finding out. No one knew why this baby had been abandoned, and DSS was not taking any chances that someone might change his mind and attempt to retrieve her. Gracie was moving, and I would not know her whereabouts.

I tried to put thoughts of homes like the Youngs' (one of Danny's first foster homes) out of my mind, but it wasn't easy. I had been doing foster care for only a few years then, but long enough to know that parents, and foster parents, can, and do, hurt babies. The Youngs had bathed Danny in ice water for wetting his bed and made him ride home from a shopping excursion in the trunk of their car because he had wet his pants during the trip. Their home was closed to foster care because of the abuse, but I knew it wasn't the only terrible home out there. There was always the chance, albeit a small one, that Gracie would end up someplace where she would be left crying in a crib and wondering where we had gone.

After a few days, though, I knew I had to move on. I had to if I was going to continue to foster and stay sane. I still wept when I found one of Gracie's tiny booties under the couch, and Angie, of course, felt awful, but we were all sleeping a bit more and starting to feel human again. And once Gracie left and I could think again, I remembered something that happened the previous summer that I had conveniently forgotten.

Across the state, a foster mother had returned from a shopping trip with a slew of kids in tow. She had a couple of children over the limit. While she unloaded groceries, she asked her eleven-year-old foster child to put the five-month-old foster child in her crib. A few hours went by before the mother realized the baby should have been up. She went to check but found the crib empty. Frantic, she searched the house. The child was found, thirty minutes later, dead, in her infant seat, still in the hot, enclosed car.

Negligence, everyone cried! How could she forget a baby? All of the children were pulled from her home, and she lost her license and her reputation. She was very lucky not to go to jail. People, including me, were quick to judge and second-guess, but after struggling with too many needy kids I have a picture of how it could have happened.

Mom gets home, a bit frazzled. She spent too much time at the market again, and Todd threw a tantrum. She had a dozen bags to carry in, and the phone was already ringing. Mom asks her little girl to carry in the baby, just as I have asked Neddy or Ben to carry in a baby for me. The child doesn't hear or forgets. Mom puts away the groceries and returns some calls, grateful the baby is taking such a good nap. She hangs out some laundry and passes out six cups of juice. When she glances at the clock, she's amazed to find out that nearly two hours have passed. I can feel her panic when she looks in the empty crib. She knows but she can't bear to know. In an instant, with one faulty decision, her life is irrevocably altered. She will never be the same again.

The department is good at begging, cajoling, pleading with homes to take another child, not because social workers are stupid, evil people. They're not. They are usually good people who have an impossible job to do. They must find families to take children, and there are more children than beds. It's a simple matter of math.

The solution, of course, is to recruit more homes. But how do we do that? Few people are really equipped to deal with the behavior of traumatized children, and the support for those that do is minimal. Respite is difficult to access. Even child care is hard to find for kids who have tantrums and need constant supervision. People fear the influence of these kids on their own children, many of whom wouldn't tolerate the intrusion in their lives. A lot of children from troubled backgrounds have huge problems in school, and a lot of systems are less than gracious about accommodating them.

It comes as no surprise that finding families willing to open their doors to the rigors of foster parenting is so hard. Fostering means knowing about things most of us would prefer to forget. It means recognizing that our best is often not good enough. It means only knowing the difficult beginnings of a story and being forced to imagine the end. It means loving children who will ultimately leave us, then drying our tears and letting ourselves love again.

Chapter

Four

Bruce and I had just recovered from Gracie's leaving when Tyler left as well. I tried to muster some enthusiasm for his return home to his parents, but I just couldn't feel good about it. He had spent nine months with us and had made so little progress. He could now count to five and dress himself. He could brush his teeth and pick up his blocks, but about the big problem, controlling his urge to hurt himself, he had really learned nothing. His forehead still sported that same purple, head-thumping bruise. I had learned what his triggers were and we had gotten pretty good at avoiding them, but several times a week, some small thing would set him off and he would fall to the floor and begin banging his head against it. Nothing I had found for him—not therapy, not medication, not structure, not patience—changed the history that made Tyler the very damaged little boy that he was.

I didn't feel great about Ty's parents either. They needed so

much, and social services had so pathetically little to offer. I wondered if there was anyone who genuinely believed that a parenting
course and some couples counseling was likely to change the dynamics of a family that had known generations of poverty, incest,
substance abuse, and violence. What this couple needed was time,
time, and more time to make any skills they picked up a real part
of their repertoire of behaviors. And time was the one thing Tyler
didn't have. A year was a third of his life. While his parents attempted to learn the skills they should have picked up as children,
Tyler jumped from a toddler to a preschooler. He made new friends
and formed new attachments. He needed to go home soon or not
at all. It wasn't Tyler's fault that his parents weren't ready.

The heartbreaking part was that I knew that Lila, his mother,
was really motivated to change. She so wanted things to be different for her family. When she came to pick up Tyler for a visit, she
sometimes looked around my living room with a wistfulness that
was painful in its longing. She looked at my kind, caring husband;
my sweet, normal children; my photographs of holiday parties and
family ski trips; and she knew that my life would never be hers. I
wished I had had the courage to ask her if she thought that she had
been cheated by foster care or if she thought it had helped at all.

Caring for Tyler was the first hint I had that fostering would
often offer only the illusion of help for a family. To foster meant
learning to be satisfied with giving Band-Aids to children and families who needed intensive care. In those first years, I believed that
each time things went wrong for families it was some sort of fluke,
that the next time it would surely be different, but it seldom was.

When Tyler went home, a selfish part of me was somewhat relieved. He was an expensive kid in terms of time and energy. Each

tantrum put everything else on hold and left nothing extra for the others. Lucy, Dan, and Karen all needed so much, but they had to be satisfied with the leftovers. With Ty gone, I had grandiose plans. I would spend more time on Lucy's academics. I would come up with a plan for improving Danny's nonexistent social skills. I would finally address Karen's intense separation anxiety.

I had plans all right. What I didn't plan on was Sara.

It was like a sickness to me, this inability to say no or recognize my limits. Even as Susan, the social worker charged with Sara's initial placement, told me about this girl, I was rehearsing how I was going to refuse. A child who had been tortured and sexually abused by every adult in her life was obviously a bit more than I was prepared to deal with, especially with Dan's problems. A six-year-old with a police record for breaking and entering? Out of control at home and at school? Three hospitalizations for failure to thrive? Of course not.

But somewhere between my brain and my mouth the "no" mis-fired. My initial feeling of fear turned into excitement, my anger metamorphosed into hope, and my planned-upon refusal vanished, replaced by an oh-so-casual "Sure. No problem. When should I expect her?"

Susan chuckled. "You're a glutton for punishment. The worker is Nora Roberts. She'll bring her by in an hour or so."

As a foster parent there are moments that remain frozen in memory. For me, meeting Sara remains one of the most vivid. I first remember seeing her standing just inside the kitchen door. She was far smaller than I expected, not just thin, although she was certainly that, but petite, with a mass of tangled hair so dirty that the color was undeterminable—perhaps blond, perhaps brown.

Her eyes were startling—a tawny brown with flecks of pure green. Nothing she wore fit properly. Her dress was too large and her sweater too small. In spite of the icy, late February weather, she wore no coat, no gloves, and no boots. Several holes dotted dark woolen tights, and her toes poked through the tips of her sneakers. She could have been a Send This Kid to Camp poster child.

There was something feral about her but something dignified as well in the way she held her tiny body rigid and refused to look at me when I knelt to face her. "Hello, Sara," I said. "We're glad you're going to be with us. After we say good-bye to Nora, I'll show you your room." Sara turned her head to avoid my eyes and deliberately pulled away. She marched across the room and wedged her body into a small space between the wall and a corner cabinet. She pulled her knees up to her chin, her dress over her feet, and her sweater over her head.

For a moment, my stomach muscles tightened. I wondered what I would do if she never came out of that corner. She sat so still and silent, she looked quite capable of crouching there forever.

Nora looked weary. She had already delivered Sara's older brother and sister to their respective foster homes and didn't seem at all anxious to tackle a recalcitrant Sara.

"Maybe you should say good-bye and let me see to her," I suggested. "She might be more comfortable without an audience."

"If you're sure you don't mind, I'm supposed to be supervising a visit in about ten minutes and I haven't had lunch yet. Are you sure you can manage?"

I looked at Sara, still as a statue, and wasn't sure at all.

"Hey, she's only six, and I've got a hundred pounds on her. How hard can it be?"

"Good-bye, Sara," Nora then said. "I'll try to set up a visit with your mom for next week. Be a good girl, okay?" The social worker mouthed a silent "good luck" to me and slipped out the door.

I wished Nora hadn't mentioned to Sara a possible visit. All of my children lived lives defined by unpredictability and broken promises. Visits are iffy propositions at best. Parents are often no-shows. Social workers are hostage to crisis, and so much can go wrong. I would much prefer to have my kids surprised by an unexpected visit than crushed by the disappointment of a cancellation.

I longed to go to Sara. Karen was sleeping and the house was quiet. I wanted to connect with this child, reassure her that things would be better now and that no one would hurt her here. I was literally itching (I feared head lice) to wash her hair and bathe that tiny body. Above all, I wanted to feed her. I have always suspected that if foster care weren't an option, a lot of foster mothers would look for careers in the all-night diner trade.

I moved around the kitchen, occupying my hands with busy-work while keeping up a one-sided conversation.

"Let's have a snack before you look around," I said cheerfully. "I have oatmeal cookies or cheese and crackers. Do you like raisins? I don't, except in oatmeal cookies. Lucy helped me make these. Lucy is eight. You'll be sharing a room with her. She's a very nice girl. Would you prefer apple juice or milk?"

I didn't really expect Sara to answer, but I did hope she would at least look up. I had never seen a child sit so still.

We were both saved from my incessant chatter by Lucy and

Dan's return from school. For several minutes they were occupied with removing snowsuits and emptying backpacks. Dan was the first to notice Sara.

"There is a girl over there in the corner, you know." Dan's speech was always slow and lacked affect. He might have been pointing out a forgotten mitten.

"There sure is, Dan," I replied. "This is Sara. She's come to stay. Lucy, Sara will be sharing a room with you. After you eat, could you show her where she can keep her clothes and things?"

"I didn't bring no clothes. I ain't staying."

At first I thought I was hearing things. Her voice was soft and muffled beneath her sweater.

"That's ok. I have some extra things you can use until I shop for you. What's your favorite color?"

Sara didn't answer, but she did pull her sweater down over her knees. I thought it best to behave as though having a little girl tucked in the corner of my kitchen was not unusual in the least.

"Do you want some cookies and milk?" I asked her. "Better hurry up or they'll all be gone."

Sara didn't answer, but she did, ever so slowly, ease her body out of her nook. She walked rather warily to the spot next to Lucy where I had set her cookies, picked them up, and attempted to retreat again.

"Not so fast, kiddo. If you want to eat, you sit at the table."

I was careful not to grab her, but I did put my hand on Sara's arm, and even that small movement caused her to flinch.

That flinch spoke volumes about Sara's life. I spoke very softly to her.

"No one is going to hurt you. We don't have a lot of rules here but we do have a few. The biggest one is that, in this house, everyone is safe. You are not allowed to hurt yourself or anyone else, and no one will hurt you. Another rule is that we eat at the table. Can you do that now, or would you rather wait until supper and try again?"

Poor Sara. She really hated to give in and join the others, but she was loathe to give up those cookies. I was gambling that an empty stomach would win in her battle to save face, but I was only partly right.

"Fine, I'll sit at the goddamn table." She jerked her arm away from me, flopped into her chair, and stuffed a cookie into her mouth. Sara was clearly some kid. She managed, with one cuss word, to salvage both her dignity and her cookie.

The older kids arrived home, all talking at once, but fell silent when they spied Sara. I couldn't blame them. They were used to finding some pretty grubby kids at the kitchen table, but Sara was unusual, even by our standards. Ben, the kindest and most tender-hearted of my kids, spoke up first.

"Well, who do we have here? A new Avon lady?"

He meant to be funny and he certainly didn't intend to offend, but Sara, undoubtedly feeling a bit under siege because of the sheer numbers of bodies surrounding her, took offense. Her anger was evident in her folded arms, clenched jaw, and hostile green eyes.

Neddy, bless her, saw how upset Sara was, and took over.

"Has anyone showed you your room yet? No? Come on, then. Do you like New Kids? I have a poster you can hang on your wall."

Like all little girls, Sara was unable to resist attention from a teenager. She gave Ben a withering look, stuck her nose in the air, and stalked off.

"Well, what do you think?" I said to the room in general. "Cute, huh?"

"Yeah, right. Give her a bath and ask me later," Nathan said. "What's with the hair? She looks like one of those kids raised by wolves."

"Don't be mean," I said. "She's had a very tough life. Hygiene probably wasn't high on the list of priorities for her."

"You can say that again. She smells pretty rank."

Sara did smell, but I hoped the younger kids hadn't noticed. Lucy wouldn't say anything but Danny would, and I was fairly certain that Sara, small as she was, might retaliate with her fists if provoked. So far, although I had had several kids who, like Tyler, hurt themselves, I hadn't had anyone who was aggressive to the other kids. It was one of the few behaviors Bruce was not likely to tolerate.

I sent Angie to see to Karen while I went through the boxes in the attic looking for clothes and trying to figure out exactly how I was going to explain Sara to Bruce. In general, I made the decision about which kids we took and which kids seemed beyond us, just by virtue of the fact that I was home and Bruce wasn't. But we did have an understanding about what we wanted. We were a family. We weren't a psychiatric hospital and didn't want to be one. An unfortunate number of kids had such overwhelming problems that a hospital or a residential placement was the only way to meet their needs. Dan was borderline. As long as he was supervised he did all right, but we were all finding ourselves pretty worn down after eighteen months of that level of care. The time was rapidly approaching when Danny was going to need more than we had to offer, and the last thing we needed or wanted was another kid as hard.

At the very least, I wanted to get Sara washed and in clean clothes before I presented her as a fait accompli to my unsuspecting spouse.

I hit the jackpot in the attic. I found the boxes of clothes that I had packed away when Angie was little. As our first little girl after three sons, Angie had been deluged with more dresses and nighties and pretty hair ribbons than any kid could ever use, and I had saved all of it.

"Hey, Sara," I yelled down the stairs. "Come see what I found."

I dumped the contents of the first large box on the bed that was to be Sara's and waited for her to dig in. But unlike most kids, Sara held back. She fingered the folds of a beautiful green velvet dress that Angie had worn for her first Christmas with us ever so briefly before letting it fall back onto the bed.

"This stuff ain't mine. I ain't wearin' it. I want my own stuff."

She had a point. Every foster family I knew kept a stash of clothes on hand. Most of us found it a lot more time and cost effective than rushing out to shop every time a child showed up. Our clothing allowance of fifty dollars for each child every three months basically could keep a child in socks, underwear, pajamas, and not much else. The rest came out of our pockets. Bruce made a good living, but even his generous salary would have been stretched if I bought all new things each time a child moved in. Realistically, we had to use a lot of secondhand clothes. Most kids didn't mind, but Sara wasn't most kids.

"I don't blame you, Sara," I told her. "I'd want my own stuff too.

But for now, this will have to do. These overalls are pretty. Would you like to try them on?"

Sara ignored the question.

"Do you got a man here?"

"A man? Do you mean a husband, a dad?"

Sara nodded.

"We sure do. His name is Bruce and he's very nice."

"Is he staying?"

Very few of my foster children ever had the experience of men who were more than transient entities. Even fewer experienced these men in any positive way. Men came, were mean to a greater or lesser degree, then they disappeared, only to be replaced by a new man. Sara's question was not only legitimate; it made perfect sense in the world she knew.

"He is staying, Sara. We've been together a long, long time. He's young Bruce's dad and Ben, Nathan, Neddy, and Angie's dad. He'll be here as long as we're all still alive. Once you get to know him, I think you'll like him. You'll be glad he's here."

"I won't like him. I'll wish he was dead."

Sara's words were chilling, not just for what she said but also for the way she said it—coldly and with certainty.

Karen was crawling around the room, examining toys and shoes that were usually off-limits to her. I picked her up, inhaling her sweet baby scent and smoothing her cap of golden curls. It was suddenly an absolute necessity that I hold her very close, that I know she was safe, if only for a moment.

"Come on, Sara. It's nearly time for me to get dinner on, and you need a bath. Do you want to pick out some clothes, or do you want me to?"

"I can pick them out. I'm not a baby. But I ain't taking no bath here."

With only a bit of discussion we came up with an acceptable outfit, right down to socks, panties, and sneakers. I laid out all the makings for a rather spectacular bath: lavender bubble bath, a fluffy towel, shampoo and conditioner, even some of my treasured English after-bath lotion. Sara watched me fill the tub, her eyes so wide that the white showed nearly all around.

"Come on, honey. Let me help you with your dress . . ."

The kick caught me completely off guard. I could only be grateful that Sara was barefoot and scrawny. Even so, she got me in that vulnerable spot right below my knee.

"I said I ain't taking no bath."

Sara turned and fled the bathroom, heading straight for the kitchen door. Which was why Bruce's first glimpse of her was not of the well-scrubbed little girl I intended it to be, but rather one of a filthy wild child streaking out the door, heading for parts unknown.

Bruce managed to snag her around the waist in time to prevent her from escaping altogether. Sara was howling, Bruce was struggling to hold on to her, all of the other kids crowded around to see what the hubbub was, and I was trying to introduce Sara over the din—hardly an auspicious beginning.

My long-suffering husband barely raised an eyebrow before he unceremoniously handed Sara back to me, poured himself a cup of coffee, and escaped to the den.

"All right," I yelled in what my kids referred to as the voice of doom. "I want everybody to go find something quiet to do. I want one half hour with no interruptions. Understand? If anyone comes near me in the next thirty minutes he had better be on fire. Otherwise he's on dishes for one week. Now scoot. Not you, Sara. You're getting a bath."

Everyone disappeared (for our crew, dishes are major), and I hauled Sara into the bathroom. I helped her get off her sweater and her dress. She reluctantly removed her tights. She was wearing no undershirt and no panties. Once again, I was thrown by the things I take for granted—things like underwear and shoes that fit. Until I became a foster parent, it had not occurred to me that not everyone owns a toothbrush.

"I'll just get dressed. I don't need a bath. I'll be a better girl. I won't kick you again. Maybe I'll take a bath tomorrow."

Sara backed up to the wall as far from me as possible. She looked so vulnerable. Old bruises dotted her arms and legs. A fresher, suspicious-looking bruise marred her thigh. I might have asked another child how it got there, but I didn't ask Sara.

So often with my children, I am acting on instinct. What worked for one kid might be all wrong for another. Somehow, I suspected that Sara couldn't take a direct confrontation. She needed to feel a modicum of control.

"I'm going to hold your hand. Can you just put your fingers in the water and tell me how it feels? I don't think it's too hot. What do you think?"

Very slowly, Sara let me lead her to the tub. She even held my hand and gingerly let her fingers slip through the bubbles and skim the surface of the water.

"It's okay, I guess."

"Do you want to put your right foot in or your left?"

She didn't answer, but she did raise one foot over the edge of the tub. With both hands holding mine, she put the other foot into the water. I could feel her tremble; her knees actually shook while she stood there.

"I can see how hard this is. You're doing a good job. Can you sit now?"

Sara managed to sit and let me bathe her, but it was like bathing a stone. She was beyond scared: Like a deer caught in a car's headlights, she was panicked into immobility.

I was as gentle with Sara as I could be, softly soaping one bony limb at a time. Bit by bit, she relaxed some, at least until it was time to wash her hair. That set off a fresh wave of protest, but she got through it stoically if not with any pleasure. She let me put some lotion on her arms although she insisted on rubbing it in herself. I worked most of the tangles in her hair out with my fingers while she was in the tub so all that was left after she dressed was the fun part. I combed and braided and set off her truly beautiful hair with perky pink bows. When I was finished, she looked adorable. She turned slowly in front of the full-length mirror, admiring herself from every angle.

I led Sara into the living room, where I could hear Bruce with the younger children. Angie was perched on the arms of his recliner. Dan sat near his feet. Lucy was as close to him as she could be without actually touching him. Her face positively glowed while she showed him her latest bird book. Bruce is an avid bird-watcher, and Lucy had chosen this subject to connect with him. Karen, as usual, snuggled deep in the crook of his arms.

Bruce chose to ignore his earlier meeting with Sara. "Hi, Sara. It's very nice to meet you. I hear you're sharing a room with Lucy. I hope you like birds."

Sara sashayed over to Bruce. She walked her fingers up his blue-jeaned thigh and gave him a little pout.

"I just had a bath, and Kathy gave me new underpants."

For a moment, Bruce was speechless. Then he pushed her hand away and spoke very sharply.

"You make me very uncomfortable when you touch me like that. I'm not interested in your underwear."

Sara flushed a deep crimson and glared at Karen.

"Little suck-up," she whispered.

Supper was a strange affair. Dan finally had some competition in the eating department. Sara devoured two heaping plates of food and three glasses of milk before slowing down. In between bites, she answered questions with monosyllables. About her family, she would say nothing. The other kids quickly tired of her lack of responsiveness and ignored her, which seemed to suit Sara just fine.

Evenings in our house were always busy. Dishes, homework, and baths meant that kids were left to their own devices unless I was working directly with one of them. Bruce was beginning a project—installing a new bathroom upstairs to replace our aging one—and a good half hour went by before I realized that although I could hear Angie and Lucy playing with Karen in the living room, I hadn't heard a word from Sara and Dan in a while. I found them upstairs in what can only be described as a compromising position. They were both still dressed but doing a pretty good job nonetheless of simulating the act of sex.

I wish I could say I handled it well. I wish I had been calm and patient but I wasn't. I was furious. I was furious and shaken and angry with myself for not realizing that, given their respective histories, Dan and Sara were going to be a problem.

"Dan, get to your room, get in your pajamas, and get to bed," I snapped angrily. "What have you been told about playing like this? You know better than to be in the girls' room. Sara, you get ready for bed too. This is not okay. I'll talk to you later."

I expected Sara to come downstairs. When she hadn't by the time I helped Lucy finish her math, I went to look for her. I had recovered my composure, and I wanted to talk. Sending her to bed early was certainly not the way I wanted Sara to remember her first night with us. I was surprised to find her already in bed but wide awake and staring at the ceiling.

"What's the matter, sweetie? Can't sleep?" I asked.

"When am I going home?"

"I don't know the answer to that. There are lots of people who care about you. People like your therapist and your social worker and your lawyer. They're going to want to make sure you're going to be safe before you can go back."

"How come I got to be here, anyways?"

"Why do you think you're here?"

" 'Cause of what I told Sandra about what Bob done to me."

"Is Sandra your therapist?"

"Uh-huh. I didn't know she was going to tell nobody. I thought it was gonna be a secret. I wouldna told if I knowed she's gonna blab it."

"She didn't have a choice, Sara. Once she knew, she had to tell. Some secrets aren't for keeping."

"Do you know what he done?"

"Nobody told me." I waited a minute. "Do you want to tell me?"

"I can't tell it if you look at me."

"Are you afraid I'll think you're a bad girl?"

Sara nodded.

"Sara, lots of girls have told me stuff like this. I never think they're bad, and I never think it was their fault."

Sara was quiet for a minute.

"Sometimes Bob wants me to touch him. Ya know, down there. He likes to put it in me."

Sara fingered the quilt. It was white with small bunnies and ducks embroidered across the top.

"He says it's how people say they like each other. He says if I put my mouth on it it's like special kissing. I don't like kissing like that."

I knew I couldn't cry. If I did, Sara might never open up to me again. I couldn't afford to have her think that I needed to be taken care of. Sara had spent far too much time as a grown-up. She needed to be a little girl who could cry if she needed to.

"Bob lied, Sara. That kind of touching is only for grown-ups and only if they both want to. He told you that just to get you to do what he wanted. In this house, the grown-ups do not touch the children in their private parts, and the children don't touch the grown-ups."

"How come you made me take a bath?"

"Everybody needs a bath, Sara. I didn't do it to scare you."

"Bob likes to play with me in the tub. He plays the dunking game. He holds my head under the water and I can't breathe. I want to scream, but I can't 'cause I'm under the water. He lets me up, but I only get to take one breath and then I have to go under again. The dunking game makes him laugh."

"Did you ever tell your mom about Bob? Did she know what he did?"

"I told her, but Bob said I lied. She believed him and not me. When I get big, I'm gonna kill him."

For some reason, I didn't tell Bruce right away what Sara told me about Bob. I needed a chance to process it first, and I think I was afraid that he would think she was going to be too much for us to handle. I took a long time falling asleep on Sara's first night with us. I wondered then, as I still wonder on occasion now, just exactly what I thought I was doing, who on earth I thought I was, to even attempt the impossible, to try to reinvent a childhood for a child like Sara.

Chapter

Five

I kept a close eye on all of the children, but especially Sara, for the next few days. What I saw confirmed what I had always known but had never put into words. Children who are born into the kinds of families that Sara and Danny were born into are different in some fundamental way. It is as if they are aliens brought into a world where they cannot eat the food or drink the water. The very air that surrounds them is poison to their lungs. But because they are by nature survivors, they adapt to this environment that was never meant to be. When the air, water, and food change to what is nourishing and good, it may be too late. The need will still be there, the desire and longing, but the ability to use what is offered may be compromised.

It sounds so cynical, so hopeless, and certainly it isn't always so. Fostering has always provided enough miracles to keep hope alive, but sometimes the prospects seem pretty bleak.

And they were bleak indeed with Sara. Seeing her in a plaid jumper, with her hair in beribboned braids and a gap where a baby tooth had fallen out, it was easy to forget how very damaged she was.

At that time, it would have been such a comfort to have someone to blame, someone to point a finger at and hate. There were plenty of candidates. There was Sara's father, a vague figure whom Sara refused to comment on except to say that she wished he were dead. There was Bob, of the dunking game. And, of course, Mom, who kept choosing men over the kids. Even now, she was living with Bob, although if she had gone to the battered women's shelter, her children could have all gone with her and been kept out of foster care.

But I knew Lucy's mom, and Dan's and Karen's and Angie's and Neddy's and Tyler's. I knew that what might seem like pure evil usually has a second face, the face from a time when they too were small and hurt and no one had rescued them. They were harder to hate than you might expect.

I wasn't a social worker. I wasn't a guidance counselor or a therapist or a doctor, but being a foster mother meant taking on parts of all those roles. I was ill equipped for a good deal of what I, out of sheer necessity, attempted, but since there was so often no one else available to do what needed to be done for a child, I just muddled through, guided by not much more than good intentions.

But with Sara, I ran into an amazing bit of luck. She came to us already seeing a truly gifted therapist. It was a blessed relief to have someone I could call who always called me back and never failed to have just the information I needed to help me figure out what I should do next. Social workers knew their cases, but therapists knew their kids, and over the years I have come to rely on them more and more when I'm feeling in over my head.

And never was I over my head more than with Sara. She had a visit scheduled with her mother and her brother, and her reaction to the news was undecipherable. She seemed less pleased than wary. Although on occasion she asked about going home, she didn't seem to pine for her family.

Usually, I prefer not to know too much about the pasts of the children who come to me. So much of a kid's behavior can be the result of environment. I like to let a couple of weeks go by before I start reaching any conclusions. By then, any honeymoon is usually over, and I have a reasonable idea of what I'm dealing with. But with Sara, it didn't feel right to wait. Her behavior was so upsetting that I needed some input right away. When I saw how destructive Sara could be to herself and others, I called her therapist, Sandra Martin, and asked for some more background and for anything I could try that might be helpful.

Sandra called me right back. She was, as were all the therapists I came to know at the Child's and Family Guidance Clinic over the next several years, smart, compassionate, and intensely devoted to her clients.

"Before I tell you about Sara," she said, "I'd like you to tell me what you've seen so far. How are things going?"

I gave Sandra a general rundown. She was one of the few professionals I've encountered over the years who didn't seem subtly critical of foster homes. For a change, I didn't feel the need to explain who I was and why I was doing what I did. And from the beginning, Sandra treated me like a valuable member of Sara's team. She understood my role in Sara's life.

For the next half hour, Sandra talked. When I hung up I spent another thirty minutes sitting quietly, digesting it all. It wasn't a pretty story.

Sara was only four months old the first time she was hospitalized. The diagnosis was failure to thrive. At home, she didn't put on weight and she seemed nonresponsive to her mother. In the hospital, she did quite well. Her weight gain was rapid, and within days she was smiling and cooing for her nurses. Neither parent came to visit for the two weeks she was there. Sara went home, and the story repeated itself. Social services was called in, and Sara was enrolled in an early intervention program that sent a worker into her home twice a month. The social worker had concerns. The house was dirty, and Sara's mom had trouble controlling the older kids. But lots of houses with three little children are dirty, and not all kids are easy to manage. Sara's dad was never around.

Sara couldn't remember the first time her father raped her. She was perhaps three. Maybe she didn't have the language to tell anyone. Maybe it didn't occur to her that anyone would care. Her brother did those things to her too. So did an uncle. There was no particular reason for Sara not to accept sex as part of life for every preschooler.

Sara's sister, a victim also, finally told their mother. For a while the sexual abuse stopped, but then the beatings got worse. It may have been a relief when Sara's father starting visiting her at night again.

One day her father disappeared. Sara didn't quite understand. There had been a fight and the police had come. Sara had to talk to people. They all wanted to know about her father. But Sara didn't tell. She knew what her father said would happen if she told.

She'd get sent away to a foster home. Her father had been in lots of them and he knew. That's when Sara starting seeing Sandra.

At first she wouldn't talk, but that was all right. She and Sandra played with a dollhouse and drew pictures and read books. After a while, Sara started to trust Sandra, and Sara opened up, bit by bit. Sandra never acted surprised or angry; she was just sorry. When Bob moved into Sara's house, Sara told Sandra about him too. She told her about the dunking game and about Bob's belt and how he hit them. That was when the lady, Nora, came to Sara's house. She was nice and Sara liked her. At least she liked her until Nora did the thing Sara feared most: She took Sara and Thomas and Annie and put them all in foster homes.

Sandra clearly liked Sara. She hated being the bad guy who went to DSS with Sara's reports of abuse. But she was awfully glad that Sara seemed to be in a safe place, at least for the time being. She gave me some tips on handling some of Sara's more difficult behaviors and set up a schedule of weekly appointments to see her.

Following Sandra's advice, I didn't mention Sara's upcoming visit with her mother and brother until just before we needed to leave. I kept my tone casual, as though this was just a run-of-the-mill occurrence, but Sara wasn't fooled for an instant. She had been with us for only a few days then, and I was still finding her a tough kid to read.

"Hey, Sara," I said. "We've got a busy day planned. I need to pick up a few things in town and then stop by Nora's office. Remember when she said she would try to set up a time for you to see your family? Well, today's the day."

There was no sound, no movement at all for several seconds.

"Is he gonna be there?"

"Who, honey? Bob?"

Sara barely nodded.

"No. Bob won't be there. Just your mom and your brother."

"Where's Annie?"

I was waiting for this question, but I still didn't have an answer. Annie, Sara's twelve-year-old sister, had swallowed a bottle of aspirin on her first night in foster care. After her stomach was pumped, she was transferred to a psychiatric hospital.

"Annie's having a hard time, Sara. She's feeling pretty sad right now and pretty mad too. She needs to be with people who can help her feel better before she is ready for a visit."

Sara didn't take her eyes off my face. She had a way of looking at me that made me feel naked, and I was the first to look away.

"Mom, Danny plugged up the toilet again," Angie was calling from upstairs. One of Danny's peccadilloes was a fascination with anything that spun. He was especially drawn to the swirling water in the toilet bowl. He flushed whatever he could get his hands on often enough so that the whole process was obnoxiously routine.

This time, however, the timing was bad. In the hubbub of mops and plungers I forgot about Sara. In the fifteen minutes it took to dislodge the clog (a potholder, of all things) and mop up the water, Sara fell apart. Her target was the cat. Molly was nasty-tempered anyway, and I had no idea how Sara had managed to grab her hind legs. By the time I heard Lucy's screams and got to Sara, poor Molly was being swung in circles around the kitchen.

"Sara! Stop! Now!"

Sara did stop but not before Molly had raked her claws from the base of Sara's wrist nearly to her elbow. Sara dropped the cat and stood there, her chest heaving and a look of terror in her eyes.

This was what Bruce was worried about, what my friends had warned me about, that someday I would get a kid who wasn't just difficult or slow or depressed but one who was really crazy, and in that moment I had to accept that they all might have been right. Sara did look crazy.

"I'm sorry. I—don't hit," Sara's words tumbled over one another, choked and incoherent. Her eyes darted frantically from Angie to me and back again.

"Danny, go change your shirt. You're soaked. Karen, come see Mommy, honey. It's okay. Lucy, don't cry. You did the right thing. Angie, would you take the kids in the den and put in a movie? Donna will be here to baby-sit in a few minutes, and I need to see Sara."

Our school had in-service training that day, so Neddy and the older boys were all spending the day with friends. I dragged Sara into the room that Bruce and Nathan shared and shut the door.

I thought about letting Sara have it and really reading her the riot act, but when I turned to face her, the anger drained out of me.

She was shaking. I tried to pull her close to me, thinking that a hug might calm her down, but she resisted and I didn't force the issue.

We sat quietly for a few minutes. I tried to think of something to say that wasn't inane, but no words came to me. It's ironic really. Those of us with the least training, at the bottom of the food chain so to speak, are the ones with the day-to-day control in the lives of these kids. In a crisis like this, I have to decide how to respond.

"Can you tell me about it, Sara? What happened?"

Sara turned her head and looked out the window. So much time went by that I thought she couldn't or wouldn't answer.

When she did speak, she used a baby voice that I hadn't heard from her before.

"Once, my dad got mad and he drowned my kitten. He made me watch. We had a pool, a little pool that my grandma brought us, and my dad, he held my kitten under the water and he drowned it. I didn't cry. I don't ever cry, but I wished he didn't do it. It didn't do nothing. He was only mad at me."

I pulled Sara to me and, for a change, she let me hold her. I even thought I could feel her relax into my chest a bit. I kissed the top of her head but couldn't think of anything to say.

After a few minutes of silence I took Sara's hand and led her into the bathroom. I could hear Donna's voice in the living room with the all-too-familiar music from *The Lion King.*

"That's a bad scratch, Sara. I need to clean it up."

Sara stoically held her arm out while I washed it off and dabbed it with an antiseptic cream.

"Can I have one of those Band-Aids with the stars on 'em?"

"Sure. But Sara? I need you to promise me something. When you're scared or angry, could you try to talk to me about it? Remember when I said this was a safe house? Well, it's safe for animals too. I won't let you hurt Molly."

I put the star Band-Aid on the worst part of the scratch.

"There. Does that feel better?"

Sara gave me a look of total earnestness.

"I don't ever hurt. I'm magic. Nothing can hurt me."

The social services building in our county offers little in the way of amenities. There is one small room off a miniscule lobby that serves as a combination waiting/visitation room. It is furnished with a few tag-sale reject toys, puzzles with missing pieces, and coloring books but no crayons. There is no place to change a diaper or warm up a bottle. The only furniture is a filthy collection of hard plastic chairs. I always wondered what the families who had lost their children because of hygiene issues in their own homes thought when they saw the stained carpet that covered the floor.

But by far my biggest concern about the place is its complete lack of privacy, bespeaking a lack of respect for all of us—clients, foster families, and social workers—that is difficult to ignore. As usual, though, it is hard to point a finger at who is responsible. I wrote a couple of scathing letters to the director in Boston and got back polite and noncommittal responses. What I didn't get was an offer to paint the walls, clean the carpet, or buy new toys.

The condition of the visitation room was not on my mind when I took Sara to visit Sharon. I confess I was primarily curious about the mother who had allowed this child to be abused as she was.

Nora was not in the visitation room, but Sharon and Sara's brother, Thomas, were. The family resemblance was clear. I thought it probable that Sharon was once as pretty as Sara, although she looked like what Bruce would describe as "rode hard and put away wet." Her hair was dyed a rather shocking shade of red, and her makeup had been applied with a heavy hand. Sharon had obviously dressed up for this visit with her daughter. I suspected she didn't usually wear stockings or high heels on a Wednesday morning.

I waited for this small, splintered family to embrace, but they didn't. They all seemed uncomfortable, ill at ease in this grim little space.

"Hi, I'm Kathy," I said. "You must be Sharon."

I purposely held back from mentioning my last name. I also hadn't told Sara our address or phone number. That was information I didn't want in the hands of parents whose mental health was in question.

I used to be touched when moms shared the intimate details of their lives with me. I thought it meant they trusted me. I know better now. I learned that people who live marginal lives, where every service they receive is a gift from a society who is disgusted by them, often lose their boundaries. They know the gift of entitlement comes with a very high price tag. The price is the access to your life, the theft of your privacy. The gift will cost you your dignity.

Sharon spoke only briefly to her children. She asked how they were doing and if they liked their new families. Then she turned to me and began her story. It wasn't told with self-pity, and it wasn't offered as an apology. Telling was just what Sharon did. She needed me to hear about her own history in foster care. The details made me cringe, and I hoped she didn't think my family was like the ones she described.

"Maybe you should wait and talk about this with Nora later," I said with a glance toward Sara and Thomas. The children were engrossed in squabbling over a handheld video game Sharon had brought with her, but it was certain that they could hear every word, and this was nothing they needed to know.

"Naw. They aren't paying attention, are you, guys?"

Sara ignored the question, but Thomas stared at his mother with a pleading look.

"Anyways," Sharon continued, oblivious to Thomas's discomfort. "I went to another home after that. Actually, I was in a lot of homes. I never did stay in one for too long. It was probably my own fault that I didn't get along so well. I was always running away and cutting school and meeting up with the boys. A couple of times I went to one of those programs where they try to get you off drugs and all, but I didn't like those places. Nothin' but rules. Now how is Sara doing?"

Sharon didn't wait for an answer.

"I know she can be a tough one. Swears like a trucker. We tried washin' her mouth out with soap, but that didn't work. She's not swearing, I hope. I told her I didn't want any of that language in my home."

I thought about dead kittens and bathtub games, mystified about how swearing fit into Sharon's ideas about what was acceptable in her home.

It was always far too warm in this room. I would have loved to take off my coat. I didn't want to encourage Sharon's monologue, but I was really uncomfortable. I settled for unzipping my jacket.

"I haven't started Sara in school yet but I expect to next week," I responded, hoping to get Sharon off the subject of herself and talking to her kids instead. "She's in kindergarten, I suppose. She seems so bright. Does she like school?"

"Thomas is in third grade," Sharon said. "He goes to special help in reading and math and talks to someone about getting along better and not fighting all the time. Other than that he does really well. Sara's doing pretty good in class. She gets into trouble some, but she sure is smart. I didn't finish school myself. I wanted to, but I got knocked up with Annie when I was sixteen and got married instead. But all my kids got the same father. That's a good thing.

Frank's been gone about a year now, ever since I found out he was still messing with the girls. I'm with Bob now. The kids are all complaining about him. But Bob says you got to be strict or kids will walk all over you. I guess I'm proof of that."

Nora came into the room in time to hear that last somewhat cryptic remark, and I was spared from having to respond.

Once Nora was available to supervise the visit, I felt free to leave. The social services building is located in the hub of a busy college area. The austere, brick building stands in sharp contrast to the liveliness of the rest of the street. Outside, on this mid-April afternoon, students in shirtsleeves were taking advantage of the first warmth of the season. They milled around me, holding hands, eating ice cream at sidewalk cafés, and laughing at one another's jokes. There was the usual array of purple hair, tattoos, and body piercings, but, all in all, they looked like such a normal bunch of kids. I caught occasional snatches of conversation about term papers, movies, and the university basketball team. I'm sure these youngsters had problems of their own, but on such a beautiful day, these problems seemed faraway and unimportant.

I had so little time alone: I decided to indulge myself for the half hour I had until Sara's visit with her mother was over. I tried to enjoy my quiet time, window shopping and poking around my favorite bookstore without the distractions of ringing phones and needy children, but it was hard to quiet my mind. I was anxious to get back to Sara. Her mother didn't seem willing or able to give her much in the way of time or attention. I suspected that Nora was spending the last half of the visit exactly as I spent the first.

I arrived back at the office to find Nora struggling to keep Thomas and Sara occupied.

"Where's Sharon?"

"Bob showed up right after you left, and Sharon left with him."
Nora lowered her voice. "The visit wasn't going well anyway. In
the future, it would probably be better not to bring Sara in a dress.
She got pretty provocative with her brother, and Sharon played
right into it, laughing when Sara lifted up her skirt and started wig-
gling her fanny. And she knew she wasn't supposed to let Bob
come around. That guy gives me the creeps. The kids literally
shook when they saw him. Hey, Sara, that's not okay!"

Sara had placed a Barbie doll, a gift from her mother I assumed,
on its back with its legs in the air. She put a second adult doll between Barbie's legs and was doing far too good a job of simulating
oral sex.

"Time to go, Sara," I said firmly. "Did you schedule another
visit, Nora?"

"Visits are going to be a challenge," she answered. "Sharon and
Bob have moved over the state line, and transportation is going to
be a problem. No way I have time to go get her and bring her
back. We'll have to see what we can work out."

Sara was quiet on the ride home. She answered direct questions but volunteered nothing. I was glad for the quiet. I had some
thinking to do.

As much as I found myself drawn to Sara, I feared we would not
be able to keep her. Bruce was not going to be happy when he
heard about the incident with the cat. He was already concerned
about the sexual acting out and had made me promise that under
no circumstances would he or one of the boys be expected to stay
alone with her. I didn't know one family who did foster care who
didn't fear an unfounded accusation ruining their lives, and with a

kid like Sara, the possibility of her pointing a finger in the wrong direction was all too real. In balancing the needs of our foster children with those of our own children, Bruce and I were quite clear. Our own kids had to come first. It simply made no sense to sacrifice our kids in order to try to save somebody else's.

Then there was the problem with Danny. He and Sara were a terrible match. He was a perpetrator, and she set herself up to be a victim. They needed to be watched every second. In my honest and not-so-nice moments, I would have preferred to have Dan move on. It wasn't just that he was hard work, although he was certainly that, but it was more that after nearly two years, I was just not connected to him. For all we tried, he remained blank and unattached. I didn't need to feel love to do a good job for a child, but I did need to feel something. I wish I could claim that, when the time came to decide what to do about Danny, Bruce and I decided based solely on the best interests of all the children, but that wasn't the case. When it finally happened, the whole thing was entirely out of our control.

Chapter

Six

❖

I usually meet children on the worst day of their short, hard lives. They come to me with an entourage—social workers and therapists, doctors and teachers, advocates and attorneys—each charged with regulating a small piece of a child's life. Because the immediate needs of a child recently taken into care are so immense, I'm usually delighted to hear from anybody interested in helping. By myself, I can't do much beyond temporarily pasting a kid back together.

The caliber of the people children find themselves saddled with really matters, whether it's their social workers or their foster parents. The responsibility is scary. We hold children's lives in our hands.

It doesn't take long for the foster parent grapevine to rank everyone involved in the system, including one another, according to ability and performance. We know who the diligent attorneys and competent therapists are. We know which judges are likely to consider the best interests of the child as the primary focus and which ones have apparently never met a traumatized toddler. We are, as a group, brutal in our assessments and slow to change our minds once they are made up.

Mine is a fairly small community, with a limited pool of professionals doing the majority of the social service work. It is not at all uncommon for two kids in one foster home to have the same therapist or to find that the attorney appointed to represent a child in my home is also representing the parent of another child in my home. Boundaries and confidentiality are important issues, and nearly everyone I deal with treats them accordingly.

Dan's general bad luck held true with the attorney appointed to represent him. She was useless. She never called, and I never saw her at a case review. His social worker was good, but her options for Dan were somewhat limited. There were no services on the planet that could make it possible for him to return home. His mother was not going to be suddenly cured of mental illness, and she wasn't likely to get any brighter. Yet Dan wasn't a good candidate for adoption; his problems were the sort that would only worsen with age. At best, he was probably looking at a placement in a group home. Danny did have a wonderful therapist. She was the only professional who worked with him who seemed to see him as something other than a problem she couldn't solve. She did little things like remembering his birthday and asking about the baseball team he played on.

Dan's mother had a terrific attorney. I saw Scott Thorp often, and he was invariably respectful to Pearl while recognizing that it was not in her best interest to try to raise Dan. When I got a call from Scott telling me he had just picked up Sara's case, I couldn't have been happier. With her problems, Sara needed all the angels she could get.

Karen had a terrific attorney too. Sam Zdiarski made it a point to visit often, and he called any time he had information he thought I would be interested in. By the time Karen had been with us for nearly a year, Sam had made it clear that he believed her interests were best served by staying with us. The goal for Karen had been changed to adoption when Bonnie was unable to complete a drug rehabilitation program. All that really meant was that the department would put all of its efforts into trying to convince Bonnie to sign a surrender of her parental rights. If she refused, department workers would put together a case and go to court. Sam was pretty clear that if Bonnie were to pull herself together, she could get her child back. I don't think he expected that to happen, but he wanted Bruce and me to be prepared. Until we went to court, anything could happen.

There was never any question about whether we would adopt Karen. She felt very much like our little girl. Adoption would only legalize a situation that already existed in our hearts. But part of Sam's reluctance to be too optimistic about our chances of adopting Karen came from dealing with Bonnie's attorney, Mark Daniels, who had the reputation of being a very tough opponent and advocate. His client wanted her child back, and he was doing whatever it took to make that happen. He was unconcerned with Bonnie's dismal parental track record or her inability to take care of herself. I always felt Mark was more invested in winning his case than he was in doing the right thing for Bonnie or Karen. Now that I know a bit more about how the legal system operates I realize he was only doing his job, but at the time, I just saw him as the enemy.

By the time Sara had been with us for a month, we had settled into something of a routine. Bruce still had some reservations about the dynamics of this particular group. Danny and Sara needed constant supervision. Lucy and Karen weren't needy in the same way—I didn't worry that they would set fire to the cat—but they still deserved some undivided attention each day and seldom got enough of it. Young Bruce had moved into his own place and Nathan was looking at colleges, but the other kids needed to be ferried around to various games, lessons, and performances. I was stretched, but somehow everything got done, and I had reached a point where, in spite of the problems, I couldn't imagine our family without any of these kids.

Foster parents are not privy to the amazing amount of legal and clinical wrangling that embroils families with children in the custody of the state. Every six months we are invited to a case review so that everyone involved can compare notes and see where a case looks like it's heading. In between those reviews, a lot can happen. There are court dates and status conferences and permanency hearings. All of this is potentially life altering for a child, but, as often as not, a foster parent won't know anything unless the result is a child being sent home. Sam was better than many lawyers about keeping me informed; he knew how much we loved Karen, but he also tried to protect me and often kept meetings to himself until he could call with good, or at least not bad, news.

So I had no idea that Karen's placement with us was in danger until Sam called late on Friday evening.

"Say it ain't so, Kathy," Sam began. "Tell me you don't have a dangerous sex offender living with you."

"Sex offender! What are you talking about? Nobody lives here but me, Bruce, and the kids."

"You've got a little guy there named Danny. A kid with quite a history, from what I hear."

"They've all got quite a history, including Danny. But Karen's not at risk. I watch my kids, Sam. You know I do. What's going on? And who told you about Danny's history?"

"Well, it seems Danny's got a father who disappeared right after he was born. Dan's mother let everybody think she didn't know who the father was, but that was because she was afraid the guy's family would try to get Danny from her. The father's name is Joseph Turner. He just ran into Pearl, and she told him then that Dan was in foster care and now Joe wants visitation with Danny."

"What does any of this have to do with Karen?"

"I'm getting to that. Now Dad goes to court to ask about visitation, and the judge makes him party to the care and protection order on Danny and appoints Dad a lawyer. Guess who the lawyer is?"

"Who?"

"Mark Daniels."

"Bonnie's lawyer?"

"The same."

"So he reads Dan's file and realizes that the son of the guy he's representing lives with us."

"Right. And the record is filled with the psych reports and all the info about Dan being a budding perp. Now Bonnie's screaming that she wants Karen moved, and Mark is filing a motion. The judge is going to hear it on Monday. One of the department's key points in terminating Bonnie's rights is that Karen will suffer terribly if she loses you. Naturally, nothing would make Mark happier than having Karen move. It makes the case for returning Karen to Bonnie a lot stronger."

"He can't do that, can he?" I swallowed back the panic I could feel building. "Isn't it a conflict of interest or something? How would Dan's father feel if he found out that his lawyer was using information he got from the file to get Karen moved and it ends up getting Danny moved from the only home he's got?"

"Right now, I've got to worry about Monday. Is this kid as dangerous as he sounds?"

"I suppose he could be. If he wasn't watched."

I was trying hard not to cry. In my mind, anger battled fear, and fear was winning. I knew I was too close to the edge to think straight. "What now, Sam? Could they really take my baby?"

"She's not your baby, Kathy," Sam said softly. "If Bonnie thinks she's at risk, she can request it. You might need to make a choice. It could come down to Dan or Karen."

Bruce found me in our bedroom, sobbing into a pillow. When I finally calmed down enough to tell him what was happening, he was as angry as I but able to reason things through.

"Look," he said. "It does sound sleazy, but there's probably nothing illegal about the way Mark Daniels got the information. The important question is, What are we going to do?"

"There isn't any doubt, is there? Karen is my baby. She might have been born to Bonnie, but Bonnie can't take care of her. I'm the one who walks the floors with her when she's sick. I'm the one she comes to when she bumps her head. I feed her and change her and rock her to sleep. When she says 'mama,' she means me. In every way that matters, I'm her mother."

"And I'm her dad. But what about Dan? Do we just give up on him?"

"You make it sound like I want to get rid of him, like I don't even care."

"That's not what I mean, and you know it. I guess I'm just feeling guilty because there's really no contest, is there?"

Of course there wasn't. Even now, I try to remember it differently. I want to have been a better person. I wish I could remember fighting for Dan, but I didn't. The only thought I had was panic at the prospect of losing Karen. I would have cut off my arm, mortgaged my house, and betrayed a nine-year-old boy who had no place else to call home in order to keep her.

The next week slipped by. The house assumed the ambience of mourning, each of us dealing with a private loss. Bruce Jr. and Nate were old enough to have lives that were largely lived away from home. Dan mattered to them only on the periphery. They felt sorry for him in a general way, but his leaving wouldn't be a huge loss. Ben, who had never gotten along with Dan and who was most often the target of his destructive tendencies, was nothing but relieved. Of all our children, Ben was the kindest and the most compassionate, so I expected some guilt to creep in. But I underestimated Ben's essential honesty.

"I don't know why you think I'll feel bad," he said. "Dan's not my brother. To tell you the truth, life will be easier with him gone. I won't have to lock up my stuff, and we can live like normal people who don't have to hide the food because if we don't Dan will steal it all."

For Neddy and Angie, though, every leaving resurrected painful memories. They remembered their own pain of having to leave wherever they were staying as children and the fear of not knowing where they would be sleeping the next night. They were angry with me, at Bruce, at social services, even at Danny. As Angie so eloquently put it, "If the stupid little pervert could have just learned to keep his hands to himself, he wouldn't have needed to leave."

To Dan, I said nothing. We didn't know yet where he was going or exactly when. There seemed to be no point in talking to him until we did.

Our social worker, Susan, was, as usual, a rock. She had a gift, not just with children but also with situations. She did what I was too close to do. She looked at the whole mess from a broader perspective.

"Dan needs a place to grow up, Kathy. Did you ever expect it would be with you?"

"Not really," I answered. "I knew the time was coming when Dan was going to need more structure than we could give him. And I'll admit that I've been thinking about specializing. I really like working with sexually abused little girls. There's no way I can do that with Dan around. But I wanted any move to be planned. I wanted it to be right for him. Now he'll end up in some crummy place, and he'll bounce around. And I hate feeling like he's been had, and that jerk Mark is going to get away with it."

"Maybe not. I want to run an idea by you. Do you remember the Petersons? David and Sunny? You did that training with them."

"The earthy-crunchy people? No kids. Thought they could save the world. Didn't he repair pianos or something?"

"That's the couple. They haven't had a placement yet. They really want to take a kid who no one else wants. I know they're a bit out there, but I called them this morning and they want to meet with you and Bruce and talk about taking Dan. They've got a nice place with a big yard."

I thought I covered up my lack of enthusiasm pretty well. I had attended a four-part training with the Petersons earlier in the year and had been underwhelmed, to say the least. Sunny was a vegetarian who wasted no time letting everyone around her know that our diets were killing not just our families but the earth as well. David wore his politics on his T-shirts and his religion like a chip on his narrow shoulders. He was perpetually angry, sure that his way was the only way. I had real reservations about the Petersons being foster parents at all and more about their ability to parent Danny. They had no experience with kids in general, never mind with one like Danny. I wondered what they would do when confronted with some of his more unusual behaviors.

I really hated to see Dan become a save-the-world merit badge for some people I didn't like much, but since the list of possible families consisted of only them, I figured that I was the beggar who couldn't afford to be choosy, and agreed to meet with them the following morning.

I know that as I sat across from David and Sunny later that week, I interpreted their natural curiosity about Dan as voyeurism. I felt an amazing sense of protectiveness toward Dan. Why should people need to know about his sexual experiences with his mother's boyfriends? On the other hand, if people didn't know, how would they deal with his inability to feel pain and his sexual

inclinations toward small children as well as the myriad other social problems he was likely to present? I also felt threatened on a
personal level. It is not that I expect anyone to see my family, my
foster and adoptive children, as necessarily better than we really
are, but I do want us seen as normal in the context of our particular family. I know that much of what happens in our home is a bit
odd, but after a child has been with us, even for a short time, whatever behaviors he or she presents tend to be separate from who
that kid is as a person. Tantrums and eating disorders, panic at-
tacks, learning disabilities, and night terrors are just part of the
packaging, like curly hair or freckles. I needed Sunny and David to
have the facts, but as a point of honor, I wanted them to see Danny
in as positive a light as possible. In some crazy way I was just talking about a piece of myself.

I was honest with them but upbeat. Dan was hard work. He
could lie and steal and hoard food, and he could be aggressive and
sexual, and he needed to be watched all the time. But he loved to
be read to and he enjoyed feeling like a helper. If he was mentally
ill according to the DSM statistical manual, he was first a little boy
who needed someone to love him.

The Petersons listened, took notes, and shot raised-eyebrow
glances at each other the whole time we talked. And while they
never came right out and criticized my handling of Dan, they
asked the kind of pointed questions that made their opinions clear.

"You actually restrict the amount of food he consumes? You
mean at nine, he's not allowed to walk to school with friends? He
sleeps in diapers?"

Guiltily I answered, "Yes, but . . ." over and over, until I began to wonder if I was too strict, too controlling, too obsessive. Maybe Dan would be a different kid in a family that could offer him more opportunities for autonomy than ours had.

The plan was made for Dan to move gradually, or at least gradually as social services measures time. An afternoon, a full day, an overnight, then he would move in, all over a weeklong period.

I told Dan on a Friday, an hour before David was due to pick him up for his first visit. I didn't ask if he wanted to go; there was no point. The choice was not his to make. I tried to be clear that this wasn't his fault. We had found a place that would be better for him. He would have more attention and lots more fun. We would visit. We would always care about him.

Dan, being Dan, did not argue or question. It is the nature of foster care that one is moved, like an old sofa with a difficult-to-match pattern, from place to place, hoping that in another corner you won't look quite so shabby, quite so out of place.

The first visit with the Petersons went well, although Dan returned to us more keyed up and anxious than usual, and that evening, for the first time in over a year, he reverted to the rocking behavior he had shown when he first came to us. He talked a lot about the Petersons, referring to them as "my new mom and dad," and talking about his new room and the puppy they promised him.

I spent the next week transferring school records and getting his clothes and toys in order.

On the day of the final move, I brought everything out to our front porch. He had come to us with what he was wearing and was leaving with a bike, some books and puzzles, his trucks, and Legos. He had a better wardrobe and a toothbrush, but I wanted it to be so much more: self-esteem and a sense of family, words for how he was feeling, the ability to cry.

I didn't fall apart until the Petersons' car pulled away. My tears then were not from grief but from necessity for the grief and because, after nearly two years with us, I had only taught Dan more about what he already knew: how to say good-bye.

Chapter

Seven

❖

My tears for Dan were short-lived. Until he was gone I hadn't focused on how much time he stole from the other kids. It wasn't just
the care—the laundry and the baths and the cleaning—although
with a nine-year-old who was still not reliably toilet trained those
things were considerable. It was the constant vigilance. I didn't
realize how wearying that piece was until it disappeared. After
a week passed without Dan in the house, I even felt my anger at
Bonnie softening a bit. Behind the thick glasses and buckteeth was
an angry and dangerous little boy, one who had never connected
enough with anyone to form a conscience. Someday Dan would
hurt somebody. I couldn't blame Bonnie for not wanting his first
victim to be Karen. In my more rational and open-minded moments, I could even acknowledge my relief that someone else
made a decision I wasn't strong enough to make.

    I began that summer with a fantasy of days spent swimming at the lake near our house, cookouts on the deck, and finally finishing reading the first of the *Little House* books with Lucy and Sara. I thought I would organize my closets and paint the bathroom and read something for myself without children or trauma in the title.

I should have known better. The long, hot days and nights of summer tend to turn social workers into pinball wizards, shooting kids from place to place, never quite resolving one crisis before alarms start clanging somewhere else.

Lucy began to transition home. Ellen seemed ambivalent about the prospect, but her worker was, for a change, quite clear with her. Either Ellen took Lucy home and started taking better care of her, she mandated, or the department would step in. They wouldn't just file for temporary custody but would put Lucy on the fast track for adoption.

The threat must have scared Ellen. She kept her next two visits and asked to have Lucy for several overnights the following week.

It was hard to watch Lucy pack for that long visit. Always so shy and quiet, Lucy became animated, almost giddy. Each sentence began with "My mom says" or "When I go home." I longed to wrap her up in my arms to protect her. She was too gentle for Ellen's world. "Don't listen," I wanted to tell her. "There is more out there for you and more to life than cold beer and hot-headed men." For all I worried, knowing what Lucy was going home to, it was worse for Bruce. As Angie and Neddy grew up and away, into a world of friends and dances, and (heaven help us) boys, Lucy slipped into the empty space. Together Bruce and Lucy watched birds and built feeders and went to soccer games. Karen was his baby, but Lucy was his buddy. He did a good job of faking happiness about her return home in front of her, but I knew he was hurting.

So off Lucy went. Her social worker had approved a full-week visit, from one Sunday to the next, with Lucy's birthday falling right in the middle. If things went well, she would come back on Sunday, have a good-bye party with her friends, and return home for good on Wednesday.

A voluntary arrangement (such as the one Ellen had for Lucy) for a child's placement in foster care is inherently different from one in which the department goes to court to get custody. A lot of safeguards are missing. Ellen could give notice any time that she wished her child to be returned to her, and the department would have no option but to comply. Another problem was the lack of anyone who was looking out for Lucy's interests. A child who comes into care because of an allegation of abuse or neglect is assigned an attorney, but those in voluntary placement are not. And workers, in general, seem less invested in kids in voluntary placement. Maybe their needs don't seem as intense. So, for a number of reasons, I felt like I was throwing Lucy to the wolves with no protection at all.

Day one of her first long visit went by. Then days two and three, and I began to breathe a bit easier. Lucy loved Ellen so much. Maybe this would work out for the best.

On day four, I got to work early. I had agreed to take a three-year-old who wasn't working out in another home. I needed to pull out the toddler bed and see what I had for clothes. My mind was flitting from thought to thought. From what had I read about PTSD (post-traumatic stress disorder), it would probably be a bad idea to bunk a very young sexually abused child with volatile Sara. When I heard the phone ring downstairs, I swore a bit under my breath at the interruption and grabbed it on the tenth ring.

"Hello?"

Silence.

"Hello?"

"Kathy?"

"Yes, who is this? Ellen? Is that you?"

"I can't do it. Can you take Lucy back early? I can't do it."
Ellen's voice trailed off.

"What's wrong, Ellen? Is Lucy okay?"

"She's fine. I just can't do it. I really thought I could, but no way.
Not twenty-four/seven. I'm going nuts. I'm signing a surrender.
You and Bruce can have her. I just want to visit sometimes."

Any sympathy I had ever felt for Ellen evaporated, replaced
by fury at the cavalier way in which she had just offered me her
little girl.

"Look, there's a whole lot more to this than just giving Lucy to
us. You need to talk to your worker, and we need to talk too. Do
you want me to come get Lucy?"

"No, I can bring her back. I'm heading in that direction anyway. I'm going camping in Maine with some friends. I think I need
some time to regroup and get my thoughts together. My therapist
says I can't take care of anyone else until I learn to take better care
of myself. That makes sense, right? She says I'm having a hard time
parenting because nobody ever took care of me. She says I need to
be my own best friend. So I think it's important for me to spend
time with my friends. You know what I mean?"

Unfortunately, I knew exactly what Ellen meant. She meant
that four days of playing mommy was quite enough, thank you,
and Ellen was ready to party. The rest was just so much psycho-
babble, hauled out to justify dumping her kid again. Here was the

way Ellen would do the dance. She would spend a week with her friends and come back refreshed and ready to be a parent, at least until the next party. Then she would abandon Lucy to foster care under the pretense of "needing a break."

In spite of her social worker's threats, Ellen didn't have much to worry about. Getting Lucy on the adoption tract would be harder than it looked. Ellen was neglectful, but she never really put Lucy at risk. Her drug and alcohol use never stepped over the line into addiction. If Ellen decided to fight the department's action, getting a judge to terminate parental rights would be an uphill battle. And it would put Lucy in the terrible position of being not really one thing or the other: not home but not adopted. She would have the worst of fates; her childhood lived in the limbo of foster care.

"Tell Lucy we're waiting for her and we'll see her soon," I said, replacing the phone very gently in the cradle, a bit ashamed of my childish urge to slam it down.

Work is always an antidote for me when I'm feeling over-whelmed. Sorting socks and sorting thoughts seem to go together, and there is nothing like scrubbing a floor for getting rid of frus-tration. By the time Ellen arrived with Lucy, nearly two hours after her phone call, my bathroom sparkled, and for the first time in weeks, the clothes basket was empty.

I managed to pull off a smile when I greeted Lucy, but it wasn't easy. She looked ghastly. She was fair skinned anyway, but now deep purple smudges under both eyes made her face look bleached. Even her lips lacked much color other than a faint rim of green. Her hair hung in limp tangles, and her clothes, raggedy things I had never seen before, looked slept in.

"Hey, kiddo, I'm so glad to see you. It's been way too quiet around here," I said, my voice assuming a false heartiness that usually spells trouble for kids. The effect was not lost on Lucy, and she looked warily from her mother to me before she spoke.

"My stomach hurts, Kathy. Could I have something to eat?"

Lucy was painfully shy. In all her months with us, I could not recall her ever asking for anything, even a glass of water, without me prompting her. For her to ask for something to eat before she even said hello was an event.

"Of course, sweetie. Would you like a peanut butter sandwich?"

"Could I please have something else?"

Now I was really flummoxed. It was a family joke that Lucy would make an excellent world traveler because she was so invariably polite that she would eat a plate of pig's eyeballs rather than risk offending. I had never known her to request something different from what she was offered.

"You can have whatever you like. Do you feel all right?"

"She's just carsick. It's a long ride," Ellen said.

Lucy glanced uneasily from her mother to me.

"I'm okay. I'm just hungry."

"Gotta go, baby. Give Mom a kiss and think good thoughts. I'll call tonight before you go to bed."

Lucy watched from the kitchen window as Ellen pulled out of the driveway. I stayed busy, pulling leftover spaghetti from the refrigerator while keeping an eye on Lucy. She sat at the table, her shoulders slumped and her hands folded loosely in her lap. Karen toddled around the kitchen, trying to capture Lucy's attention with baby chatter and drooly kisses, but Lucy's eyes remained riveted to an invisible spot on the floor.

Sara bounded into the house with Angie hot on her heels, and for a few minutes things seemed nearly normal. Angie and Sara argued, Karen fell and put her tooth through her lip, and the phone rang. I mopped up blood with one hand, picked up the phone with the other, and silenced the girls with a sharp glare. While Sara stomped upstairs, Angie turned her attention to Lucy.

Some of Lucy's apathy dissipated in the face of warmed-up leftovers and Angie's gentle persistence. By the time Lucy finished a glass of milk and a second bowl of spaghetti, she looked considerably better and was, if not exactly chatty, at least willing to respond to a direct question.

Lucy spent the whole afternoon in a gloomy mood. Even an evening trip to the lake failed to energize her much. Still, I put off any attempt to talk until the younger children were in bed and I was alone with her in the hush of a darkened room.

Talking with children is all about timing. Insisting on too much intimacy before they are ready will just put them off. If you wait too long, you risk losing the moment. I didn't ask Lucy what was wrong. She probably didn't fully know the answer. Nor did I ask if she had had a good time with her mother. The question was too loaded for honesty. Instead, I relied on a conversation starter I used a lot with my children, a game we called "Best and Worst."

Children who have lived in chaos often don't have labels for their feelings. Things just happen to them with no one bothering to help them process it or put it in any kind of context. Because of their egocentric natures, children perceive adult events as being all about them. If the police take a parent away in handcuffs, a child doesn't understand that it happened because that parent was drunk and disorderly. A child assumes that the parent drank because of the child's misbehavior. Therefore the arrest was the child's fault. If no one talks to the child about the natural fear, anger, and embarrassment that result from watching your parent shoved into a police car, the child has nothing to do with these feelings but let them out through everyday behavior. The angry kid becomes aggressive. The sad one can't stop eating. Nothing makes me more furious than having a child come to me with a bag full of antidepressants or Ritalin but not the name of a therapist he could talk to on a regular basis. The money for therapy is there, but the kids who move around a lot have a very tough time accessing services. Social workers don't have time to do all the necessary legwork, and a lot of foster parents feel that, for fifteen dollars per child per day, it isn't their job either.

I have, however, over the years, worked with some excellent therapists who specialize in traumatized children, and I have never been adverse to outright thievery when I see them use a technique that really works. I stole the "Best and Worst" idea from Dan's therapist.

"It sure was lonely around here with you gone," I said to Lucy now. "That was the worst thing. The best thing was getting to go shopping for your birthday. We're going to have the party tomorrow night. What was the best thing about your visit with your mom?"

"The first night," Lucy answered. "My mom had all her friends over, and she bought lobster and I got a claw all to myself. Lenny let me have a sip of his beer. It was really fun, but then the neighbors complained about the noise, and the cops came and made everybody go home."

"Was that the worst thing?"

Lucy seemed lost in thought for a minute.

"No," Lucy replied. "The worst thing was when my mom and Lenny went out and I had to stay home. I know I'm old enough, but I get scared. When bad guys are on TV, I'm always afraid that they'll come to my house."

"You know, Lucy, nine really isn't old enough to stay alone, especially at night. Did your mom go out a lot?"

"I guess. Mostly every night. And I got so sick of peanut butter. But that's all we had. My mom spent all her money on my party, and then she couldn't go shopping again till the food stamps came in."

"You never showed me what your mom got you for your birthday."

"It's still in my bag. You wanna see?"

Lucy dragged her backpack from the top of her dresser. She pulled out two T-shirts. Both were black and clearly meant for a boy. One had a motorcycle on the front and the other, a deer. Neither looked new or even particularly clean. I really didn't know what to say. I suppose I seem ridiculously sexist and old fashioned, but I have yet to meet a nine-year-old girl who doesn't prefer pink and purple (preferably with glitter kittens) to boys' black shirts.

"Just once I thought she might get me something pretty," Lucy said wistfully. "Maybe something yellow."

Those sentences ripped at my heart. Lucy was such a nice little girl, and she asked for so little from Ellen—just something yellow.

"I thought the worst thing might have been coming back early," I said. (I had to resist saying "coming home early.")

"No," Lucy answered. "I didn't mind coming back. I think my mom was getting a little sick of having me around anyway."

"Why do you think that?"

"That guy, the one who drove me here—she brought him home with her one night, and I think she wanted to be with him and he didn't like having to bother with me. He made me go outside and sit on the steps so they could be alone. He said I was always underfoot."

"Well, you're not under my feet. I'm mighty glad to have you."

"Kathy?"

"What, sweetie?"

"How come my mom doesn't like me?"

I took a deep breath. It was an honest question, and it deserved an honest answer but one that would not leave Lucy feeling unloved or unlovable.

"I don't think it's about liking you, Lucy. Your mom has had a hard time. I'm not sure that she had much of a chance to learn how to be a mom."

"Am I going home?"

"I'm not sure, hon. This was your mom's chance to prove to social services that she could take care of you. Things didn't go so well. She left you alone, and she didn't feed you. She brought home strangers who might have hurt you. And she only lasted four days."

Lucy's voice took on an unfamiliar, angry edge.

"You don't have to tell. If you don't say anything I'll get to go back."

"That's not fair, Lucy. You can't tell me stuff like this and expect me to not let your worker know."

"I don't want to get adopted."

"Who said anything about getting adopted?"

"I heard you tell Sara that when kids can't go home that some-times they need to find new homes. They need to get adopted."

"I'll let you know when it's time to worry about that," I said. "Now is not the time."

I gave Lucy a quick kiss on the forehead and pulled the blan-kets up to her shoulders before I went to check on the other kids.

Karen was sleeping. Her cheeks were flushed, and damp curls lay softly around her face. She clutched her bear tightly under her chin. She was a beautiful little girl. I took a moment to trace a sil-ver strand of drool that ran from the corner of her mouth to her pillow.

Next I went to the toddler bed we had tucked under the eves. I had a second of disorientation: For the life of me I could not re-member the name of the little girl sleeping there. Who the heck was she? How had she come to be there? Then she turned to-ward me and it came flooding back. Thank goodness. Her name was Lorinda. There had been a domestic dispute that ended with Mommy in the hospital and Daddy in jail. An aunt was taking Lorinda in the morning, which was fortunate, because I had an-other toddler sleeping in the den and I needed the bed.

I went last to check on Sara. It was no surprise to find her with her eyes wide open. I checked the children often and seldom found her asleep.

"Hey, Sara," I whispered. "What are you doing awake?"

"I don't never sleep. It gives me bad dreams. I just lay awake and rest my eyes sometimes."

Sara had settled in some, but she was still a very tough kid. We had established, much to Sara's chagrin, that in this house, Bruce and I were in charge and in control. That didn't mean that Sara didn't test us many, many times a day. She had all of the really unpleasant behaviors of a seriously abused child. She soiled her pants and smeared the feces on the toilet. She scratched her face and arms until they bled. She turned up the sexual heat around any man she met. Hardest of all, she attempted to lure younger children into sexual games. This meant constant vigilance if I was to keep everyone safe. But there were bright spots too. Sara was really smart and funny in that unintentional way that some kids have. Under her rock-hard veneer she could even be sweet, and I found myself drawn to her. I would look up from some small chore sometimes and find her staring at me, as though trying to figure out exactly what game I was playing. If I smiled at her, she would give me a quick grin and return to whatever she had been doing. She had a great capacity for joy and reveled in the pleasure of experiences that most little girls take for granted. Stirring cake batter or snuggling for a story were events of great note for Sara, and her pleasure made those things special for me too.

"Well, it's time to go to sleep," I said. "Maybe if you think of something extra nice, it will help keep the bad dreams away."

"How come you like us? We ain't even your kids, but you're nice to us. Our own mothers don't even want us."

I had had this conversation before, and I never got any better at it. How do you explain poverty and drug addiction to a six-year-old? How much do children need to know about mental illness and violence? I figured that my children knew enough already. They didn't need to hear about it from me.

"It's a lucky thing that people who need each other in this world have a way of finding each other," I told her. "I'm awfully glad you're here."

"Is there really a tooth fairy?"

I'm not sure what I expected Sara to say right then, but that certainly wasn't it.

"Why do you ask? Did you lose a tooth?"

Sara reached under her pillow and pulled out a tiny, tissue-wrapped package.

"Neddy said if I put it under my pillow the tooth fairy would come and leave me a dollar. I don't want any fairy coming to my bed, but I would kinda like the dollar."

"How about this," I replied. "You give me the tooth and I'll give you the dollar, and we won't worry about the tooth fairy if you don't want to."

Sara looked vastly relieved.

I heard the phone ring downstairs. At that time of the evening it was likely to be for one of the teenagers, so I stayed upstairs, glad for a few uninterrupted moments with Sara that didn't involve a discussion about why we don't need to poke ourselves with safety pins. It was a few minutes before I noticed Bruce standing in the doorway. His face said the news was not good.

"What's the matter?" I asked in the tone of voice I usually reserved for my dentist.

"That was Miguel from hot line. Sunny and David called and asked for Dan to be picked up immediately. I guess he molested their niece, and they want him gone now."

I knew the answer before I asked the question.

"What did you tell them?"

"I said we couldn't keep him, but we'd take him for a few days until they found something."

Bruce caught my look.

"I know, Kathy, but what could I do? Nobody else is going to take him, and he would get eaten alive in the shelter. Really. He's got no place else to go."

Chapter

Eight

❖

Bruce was right. There wasn't any place else for Danny to go. So back he came, the same little boy we said good-bye to six weeks earlier but not the same at all.

Every time a child moves from one home, from one set of care-givers, to another, no matter how necessary the move, no matter how kind or well intentioned the movers, a piece of him is lost. And in the small, seemingly insignificant details of the move, that piece is often a measure of self-worth, usually from a child who hasn't any to spare.

Dan returned with his belongings stuffed into a green garbage bag. Would it have taken that much more effort to fold them and put them neatly in a box? Perhaps it would have required more than either David or Sunny could spare given what their last week with Dan had been like.

We had warned them about the food and the toileting and the

sexual problems. But all of our instructions must have sounded like the ranting of lunatic foster parents. Surely, no small boy could possibly be so damaged as to require the level of supervision that we suggested. So they treated Dan like any normal nine-year-old, allowing him to roam the neighborhood unsupervised and unprotected. The ensuing disaster was both dramatic and absolutely predictable.

Dan's food issues didn't diminish with an open-door policy in the kitchen. They escalated until he was eating nearly constantly. Still, he was never quite full, and the neighbors were disgusted to find him rummaging through their garbage. He didn't stop soiling and wetting himself just because Sunny asked him nicely to use the bathroom and offered him a new bike if he stayed clean and dry for a week. Danny just reverted to his old behavior of hiding his dirty underwear in foul little bundles around the house.

Without an adult to run interference, Dan quickly ran into trouble with the neighborhood kids. Soon, the phone at the Petersons began to ring with complaint after complaint. Dan hit, Dan kicked, Dan punched.

It's possible that the Petersons would have managed to hang on to Danny for a while longer had Dan not committed one final, unforgivable act. At a family party, he was left alone playing with a group of younger children and molested Sunny's two-year-old niece.

David barely kept the toddler's father under control while Sunny called social services and threw Dan's things together. There was no time or energy to process what had happened. Dan was just gone.

The Dan who walked in our door was subtly different than the

Dan of six weeks ago. There had always been an element of sweetness about this child that transcended even his most difficult behaviors and made it possible to tolerate and even care about him. But he returned with that gone and with an edge about him, an edge that threatened to erupt into real rage. For the first time in our nearly two-year history, I was a bit afraid of Dan.

My fear showed up in small ways and taught me something I would just as soon not have known: I set the tone in my house, and the other children took their cue about acceptable behavior from me. When I let my bad feelings about Dan show (and I did let them show far more than was good for either one of us), the other kids quickly followed suit. Kids who have issues with their own self-esteem, and all of mine did, love nothing better than to have someone they can feel superior to. Dan was the perfect target. Sara, Angie, Ben, even Lucy, went from ignoring Dan to being downright mean to him. The fault for that lay directly with me.

It was nearly eleven P.M. when Dan showed up. We bunked him in a sleeping bag on the living room floor. Under the circumstances, Bruce and I thought it best to have him sleep away from the little girls and somewhere it would be easy to keep an eye on him. Sara was the first to discover him, and her response was hardly warm.

"What's he doing here? I thought you got rid of him."

"We don't get rid of kids, Sara," I told her. "Dan went to a new home but that didn't work out. He'll be staying with us until we figure out what to do next."

"Well he stinks like pee, and I ain't gonna sit next to him."

"You'll sit where I tell you to sit and stop being rude. Danny, get some clean clothes from your bag, and I'll start the shower for you."

"I'm eating first." Dan leveled a glare at me.

"A shower first, then you can eat."

"No." Dan's "no" sounded like he meant it.

Dan had never openly challenged me before, and I wasn't sure what to do next. Fortunately, with Dan, there was always food to bargain with.

"I sure hope there're some eggs left when you finish your shower. If you wait much longer, there might not be."

Dan curled up his lip, but he did move toward the bathroom. Very softly I heard him mutter the word "bitch."

If I had gotten more sleep the night before, if I hadn't been facing seven kids under the age of ten stuck inside on a rainy day, if I hadn't been so damn angry about the whole sorry mess, I would have probably let it go. But I was tired and tense and frustrated, and I didn't let it go.

"Look. I didn't wet the bed, you did. I don't smell, you do. And I didn't molest that kid. You did. Now go shower!"

My voice got louder with each sentence, and by the time I finished I was really yelling. My older kids seemed only mildly surprised by my tirade, but the two little ones who hardly knew me must have thought they had been dropped off right in the middle of the asylum and that, once again, the inmates were in charge.

There I stood, in all my glory, toe to toe with a retarded nine-year-old. Poor Lorinda sobbed in Angie's arms. Lucy sucked on her bottom lip and tried to comfort Tammy, who was only two and had arrived the afternoon before. Bruce was long gone, and it was just as well. This was hardly my finest hour.

I wish I could say that things looked up after that difficult first morning, but they really didn't. The final days of summer slipped by, marred by my anger, which hopped around from Dan to the Petersons to social services to myself like errant puffs of popcorn. That anger is what I remember most about the summer, but there are other memories too, and I can still haul them out when I need a smile.

I took the kids to the lake one afternoon in an effort to escape the worst of the August heat. Dan didn't like the water, but he enjoyed digging in the sand. Sara hated all bodies of water, so she joined Dan with pails and shovels on the beach. For a change, their play seemed like just play, with none of the violence or sexual misbehavior that usually marked their time together. Lucy, Angie, and Neddy all loved the water, and the lake was their favorite place. Karen, Lorinda, and Tammy were best buddies, splashing one another in the shallows and competing for my attention with wet, sandy hugs. We hated to leave, but dark clouds on the horizon looked like trouble. I gathered up towels, beach balls, and assorted children for the short trip home. The first drops of rain were splattering on the windshield by the time we arrived. I let the wet towels wait while the kids and I enjoyed a spectacular thunderstorm. Like most storms in late summer, it was brief but vivid, followed by a dramatic drop in temperature and dazzling sunshine.

"Look, Kathy, a rainbow!" Lucy called from the porch. Sure enough, a brilliant double rainbow hung in the sky behind the barn.

All the children gathered in the backyard. Angie stood with her arms around Lucy's shoulders, her chin resting on the top of Lucy's head. Neddy balanced Karen on one hip and with her free hand pulled Tammy to her side. Sara knelt in the wet grass, slightly apart from the others, her mouth agape, showing the gap where

her front tooth used to sit. Dan walked to where I stood holding Lorinda. After a moment of silence he reached up and gently
slipped his hand into mine.

It was so short, a still life where history was forgotten and all of
the kids were just kids, looking at a rainbow.

That one day was wonderful, but it wasn't enough to sustain us.
Danny's problems still made him too much of a threat to the other
children, and he had to leave.

We hung on for a couple of weeks, probably longer than we
should have. Bruce and I hoped for a miracle, for some family to
come forward who might be right for Dan. But there was no miracle and no family. In desperation, Dan's social worker referred him
for specialized foster care.

Specialized-care agencies were created in response to the growing number of kids who don't fit in traditional foster care. The kids
they take are usually older and often have been hospitalized for
psychiatric problems or have had run-ins with the law. Specialized
homes take in far fewer children per home and get paid nearly three
times as much as a regular home.

There is some animosity between the two. Many foster parents
feel that specialized homes get paid an extraordinary amount of
money for doing the same work with the same kids that we do
every day. Their success rates are not better, and they move kids
just as often. But the specialized homes believe they deserve more
money because they take the kids that no one else can handle, kids
who have been screwed up in regular foster care. There is an element of truth in both arguments.

Because of Dan's emergency status, he was moved to the top of
the waiting list for specialized care, and after a relatively short

time we were once again packing him up for another move. This time there was no transition and no preparation, no sense of an advantage or a new beginning. It felt like Dan was just bouncing from one nowhere to another.

All of us were in a state of flux that summer. My older children were moving into young adulthood and away from home. Neddy had entered what was proving to be a very rocky adolescence, and my foster children would all find themselves in some crisis of transition over these months.

Ellen returned home from her camping trip to find that her social worker had kept her word: She had filed and obtained a care and protection order in court. At the same time she also had filed for a permanency hearing. That too was allowed, and Lucy went from a short-term voluntary placement in foster care straight to the fast track for adoption. Ellen, who two weeks earlier had offered me full custody of her daughter, was furious. The state appointed a hotshot young feminist attorney for her, and together they launched a full-scale effort to wrestle custody of Lucy away from social services. But the department wasn't budging. They thought that Ellen would cave in and sign a surrender rather than face a trial. Even if she didn't, the social services attorney was certain there was enough evidence of persistent neglect to win in trial. Visitation was decreased to the minimum of an hour once a month, supervised in the office.

The job of telling Lucy about the change in her life fell to me. It wasn't a job I wanted or felt at all qualified to do. But Lucy had no real relationship with her social worker, and this certainly didn't feel like news that should come from a virtual stranger.

Bruce took the younger children to the lake so I could have

some private time with Lucy. I thought about making popcorn or ice cream cones, but I decided against it. Really, how do you set the stage to break a kid's heart?

Lucy and I sat next to each other on the sofa. The late afternoon sun slanted across the living room. I searched around for some small talk, some lead-in, but came up blank. There was nothing to do but jump in.

"Lucy, do you remember when we talked about all of the people who care about you? You have a social worker, and now you have a lawyer. You have Bruce and me."

"I have my mom too. She loves me best of everybody." Lucy's voice held a note of urgency. She so wanted to believe in her mom.

"She does love you, Lucy. But moms need more than love. They need to know how to take care of their kids. They need to put their kids ahead of other people. That's the part your mom has had a hard time with. She doesn't always remember to put you first. She doesn't always keep you safe. That makes your social worker worry. She wonders if it might not be better if your mom grew up some more before she tries to be a parent."

"You mean I have to stay in a foster home longer? I thought I could start school at home."

"That's the problem," I replied. "You need a home now. You need a family to grow up with. You don't have time to wait for your mom to grow up."

Lucy's chin dropped nearly to her chest, and it was impossible to see her face. I wasn't sure she was crying until her shoulders began to jerk and she buried her face in her hands.

"You know what I'm talking about, don't you?"

Lucy's only answer was a small, strangled sob. I put my hand on her arm and tried to move her toward me, but she yanked away, isolated in pure misery.

I let her cry, not because it was best but simply because I had no idea what to do next. Several minutes went by before she finally spoke.

"I don't want to get adopted."

"I don't blame you. It must feel pretty scary. But remember how scared you were when you came here? You barely spoke for the first week. And now, we care about each other. We may not be related, but we've made a family. That can happen again. You can love another family and still love your mom."

"Why can't I just stay here? I could just be your foster kid till my mom grows up. I don't care if it takes a while. I'll wait. I don't even know anybody who's adopted."

"Sure you do. Angie and Neddy are adopted. They started out as foster kids. Their mom couldn't pull it together for them either, and they needed a new family."

"But it's different for them. They don't seem adopted, or foster. They seem real."

"You're real too, Lucy. Not foster or adopted. Those are just labels, not who you really are."

"I don't know who I am. I don't feel like anybody anymore. I just want to go home."

"You will go home, Lucy. It won't be the home you expected or wished for, but it will be a forever home just for you."

It was odd to be saying these things to Lucy and for more than one reason. The first and most important one was that, for all of my big talk, there were no guarantees about Lucy's future. The process was more than a bit complicated. Lucy would be assigned an adoption worker. Depending on caseloads, this could take two weeks or six months. This worker would try to match Lucy up with a family who wanted to adopt. At the same time, the social services legal staff would be preparing their case for court. A court date could be a year in the future. Lucy would in all probability be in a preadoptive home with no guarantee about the outcome of a trial. Both Lucy and her new family would be trying to bond and connect long before Ellen's rights were terminated.

The second reason was strictly personal: Bruce wanted to keep Lucy. The rest of the kids, Angie in particular, would have gladly welcomed her as a sister. I think that Lucy would have been grateful to have her future settled. And I suspected that Ellen would have signed a surrender if we were the adoptive family. This is a painful thing for me to admit, but the one holdout in this happily-ever-after picture was me. I loved Lucy in the same general way I loved all of my foster kids. I liked who she was and how she managed in the world. But no matter how hard I tried, I couldn't feel the same sense of "mineness" that I felt for Neddy and Angie and Karen. And I believed Lucy not only needed that but also deserved it. She was entitled to a mother who felt about her the way I felt about Karen. She was meant to be someone's beloved child, and wishing it were so didn't make her mine.

Bruce understood. He even agreed with me that adopting Lucy would probably not be in her best interests. He never made me feel guilty or selfish. But as I so often found, there was no way to do what I do, day in and day out, without feeling enormous guilt over the things I couldn't give these children.

Lucy was not my only child with a life in transition. Sara's was in a holding pattern too. Her mother was able to maintain a very tentative hold on herself when her children were with her, but once they were removed she quickly spiraled out of control.

In the six months Sara had been with us, Sharon had moved to a neighboring state with Bob, gone to a battered women's shelter, attempted suicide, been hospitalized, and then moved in with yet another man. The last Nora heard, Sharon was down South, maybe Florida, maybe Texas. She had that one visit with her children, and then she disappeared from their lives. The court process for a termination of parental rights had already been set in motion. It would have been no contest, since the children had effectively been abandoned, except that Sara's father was fighting. He was willing to sign surrenders on his older children, but he wanted Sara. Because Sara had never been able to testify in court about the abuse, physical or sexual, that she had endured at his hands, he had never been arrested, much less convicted of a crime. The man was no fool. He knew Sara would never be able to talk in a room full of strangers about what he had done to her. He wanted his day in court, and he wanted his daughter.

Sara was the only child I ever met who seemed completely un-attached to either one of her parents or to any of her siblings. She never made pictures for them or asked for them when she was sick. She only rarely questioned why they had disappeared so completely from her life. She never once asked when she might have another visit. It was more than a little odd and very worrisome. At-tachment disorders were something about which I knew very little, but Sara was giving me a crash course. She was much like Dan in her lack of conscience and total disregard for any standard of ac-ceptable behavior. She did all the same things Dan did, from hurt-ing animals to abusing smaller children. She clawed her skin until she drew blood and tore hair from her head, but there was one fundamental difference that made me hope for Sara in a way that I didn't hope for Dan: I believed that Sara wanted to change. I believed that she could change, and I believed that she loved me.

There was no rational explanation for those beliefs. All I had were moments, tiny snapshots of time when our gazes would lock and I glimpsed the little girl behind the angry hazel eyes. I would enter her room and catch her rocking a baby doll and crooning a little melody that I recognized as the one I sang to Karen. One damp afternoon, I took all the children into the backyard and we blew bubbles. The air was filled with hundreds of shimmering, iridescent spheres. Sara stood in the middle of this bubble blizzard, spinning slowly, with a look on her face of what I can only call rapture.

I lived for those moments. Sara was work, hard work, and she was heartache and trouble, but she was so muchs more, and that more made me wonder how I would ever let her go.

And if my worries over Sara and Danny and Lucy weren't enough, I had to contend with the constant terror of losing Karen. Bonnie was visiting again. She was in a good family shelter and, for the first time since her pregnancy with Karen, clean and sober. The goal for Karen was still adoption, and the trial was set for late October. The case for the termination of Bonnie's parental rights was only fairly strong, and in my quiet moments I had to admit that I was really scared. The standard for termination at that time was not the best interests of the child, as it is now, but rather the current fitness of the parent to care for the child. By that standard, if Bonnie remained clean and sober, if she maintained suitable housing, even if that housing was in a shelter, if she continued to visit her daughter on a regular basis, she would certainly get Karen back.

The moral dilemma for me was that, if she did all of those things, I knew she should get her child back. That was supposed to be the plan. The problem was, as it always is, one of time. Karen had been with us for over half of her life. For a good portion of that time, she didn't visit her mother on a regular basis. She had no memories of an earlier time. The only family Karen knew was our family. In all the ways that really mattered, I was her mother. Was it fair to deny Karen the opportunity to grow up with her family of biological origin because we were more stable and more affluent? On the other hand, was it fair to rip her from the family of her heart because her birth mother appeared to be pulling herself together? Would anyone be comfortable sending her home to a very fragile mother living in a shelter to avoid having her attachment to us grow even stronger? Those were the questions I wrestled with each day. And if I was not prepared to hurt Karen by moving her home, how then was I able to sleep at night knowing that I was sending Lucy to live with strangers?

I took some comfort from the knowledge that the final decision for all of this lay with people I had never met. Judges and administrators would decide the ultimate fate of these children. I could state my opinion and advocate the best I could, but in the end I would do as I was told.

And each week I was told to bring Karen to Bonnie.

It is hard to say whom the visits were hardest on. Certainly, Karen let us know how she felt about leaving me. Her screams began the moment I took her from her car seat and continued unabated while I handed her to Bonnie.

Bonnie must have suffered her own special brand of agony, trying to hold on to Karen while she screamed for her mommy to
please, please come back. I know I never dropped Karen off without retreating to my van to shed the tears I held back during those
dreadful good-byes.

It was always such a scene. Even Bonnie's support staff at the
shelter began to be a little less hostile toward me after a few weeks
of Karen's distress. It was clearly a horrible time for all of us.

During all this turmoil, I had my own social worker to call on,
a family resource worker in charge of supervising foster homes but
not individual children. Susan was more accessible to me than any
particular child's ongoing worker, and I found her a tremendous
source of support.

Ongoing workers carry huge caseloads of families in extreme
crisis, and by necessity they put their time and energy into whatever crisis calls the loudest. I was far too quick then (and still am)
to try to manage everything myself. Bruce operates in the same independent mode as I do. As a result, we were often left fumbling
for answers when we should have asked for help.

And I needed help. I wanted to do a good job with these children. My whole identity was becoming wrapped up in my ability to
handle tough kids, the kids no one else wanted. But trying to meet
the needs of such badly damaged children was beginning to deplete
my own emotional bucket. Bruce had his job as a distraction; the
older children had school. But I was in the trenches every day, and
the stress was starting to tell. The last thing I wanted was to become
the kind of foster parent who just went through the motions, the
kind who just watched children come and go, the kind who never
made a difference, the kind who never changed anything at all.

I needed a change, something to recharge my batteries, if I was going to continue caring for such needy children. Even part-time work didn't seem feasible given my schedule and the fact that my only training was in early childhood education. The last thing I wanted to do was work in a child-care setting, but I certainly needed to do something that would get me out of the house occasionally and not require changing diapers.

When Susan stopped by for her required bimonthly visit, I brought up the subject with her. She had a couple of suggestions. The first was that I take the thirty-hour training program that would certify me to lead the training program that is required of all foster and adoptive families. The training program, called MAPP (Mutual Approach to Partnership in Parenting), was designed to be led by two social workers and an experienced adoptive or foster parent. I found it hard to think of myself as experienced since I so often felt like I had no idea what I was doing, but I filled out the application when it arrived in the mail the following week anyway and was pleased to be accepted into the next class.

Susan's second idea was more of a plea than a suggestion. Each area social services office was supposed to appoint a foster parent (again, experienced) to serve as a liaison between foster parents and office staff. The liaison supported a foster parent if he was accused of abusing a foster child in his care and was also supposed to be available to assist new foster parents in obtaining information on and referrals for services for their children. The last liaison had resigned several weeks earlier, and no one had come forward to fill the slot. Since most of the liaison's work could be done over the phone, I agreed to give this a trial as well. Neither position paid much money, but each offered just the kind of release I was looking for. I would be providing a necessary service and spending time with adults, but I could set my own hours and, most important, be working with people who could understand that my children at home had to come first.

My new positions put me in the social services office for an hour or two a week. I heard a lot about what was happening on the political front that I would not otherwise have been privy to until it hit the newspaper. There was a rumor of big changes coming in the way services were going to be delivered to children and families that would have a direct impact on all of us involved in foster care. Rumors had flown before without much changing, but there was reason to believe that this time things might well be different.

Nine children had died while in state custody the previous year and eleven the year before that. Generally, foster children are the invisible orphans in an overburdened system, but ours is a small state, and twenty kids are a lot of kids to lose in twenty-four months. The deaths were responsible for the calls for reform that were being heard from all fronts on a daily basis.

This happens to most social service systems from time to time, but not much seems to really change. Part of the problem with any meaningful reform comes, I think, from the not-so-subtle sense of elitism that infects a fair number of people who have never lived the kind of marginal life that so many families do. There is a prevailing notion that people who live desperate lives, mired in poverty, drug addiction, and mental illness, should just buck up and do better. If they don't, then they clearly deserve what befalls them. Their offspring and the people charged with caring for them acquire at least a hint of guilt by association. Societal compassion is reserved for the youngest and most grievously injured children:

No one holds the battered infant accountable. But by the time those same children reach the public school system and begin gobbling up limited special education money, compassion starts to wear thin. And when the big problems of neglected and abused children emerge and the mental health and criminal justice systems get involved, even the illusion of caring for these children is gone. They transform from innocent victim to offender status as soon as they hit puberty. True reform is shackled by public perception and private sentiment about entitlement programs and the poor. Social services are expected to heal themselves but not spend too much money in the process.

That year, two pieces of reform emerged simultaneously. The number of children allowed in each foster home was reduced from eight to six. Only four of those six could be foster children. At the same time, every foster home in the state was required to undergo a complete evaluation in an effort to eliminate the truly grim ones from the roles. In one twelve-month period, five hundred homes came off the roster.

Both of these were necessary first steps, but they failed to take into account the reality of the situation. Good and bad foster homes were already swamped. There was never an empty bed. Eliminating bad homes and reducing child-to-caregiver rates sounded good in theory, but it begged the question of what we were going to do with the children.

The quick answer was to reduce the number of kids coming into care and to get the ones waiting for permanent families adopted as quickly as possible. But leaving kids in their biological homes meant plugging in services for those families that either didn't exist or had lengthy waiting lists. Often, service providers required commitments that marginal families could not comply with.

It is one thing to sit in a meeting and declare that the Simons family needs a parent aid and therapy, day care, and affordable housing. It is quite another to make all the referrals and work out appointments when the family has no phone, no car, and a mom who is too depressed to get out of bed. The result was that much of what everyone knew was necessary to keep a family intact remained an ideal. It existed in a dream world for a family whose problems were all too real.

Recruiting new homes was then and still remains a problem. Fostering kids considerably disrupts a family's home life. Foster parents are either saddled with the unnecessary and unwanted mantle of sainthood or seen as only slightly better than the worst of homes. Either way, no one wants to pay us much beyond compliments or insults, neither of which takes care of the mortgage.

Which brings us to the subject of money. It is a subject sure to garner much discussion, no matter which end of the political spectrum you hail from.

Money means different things to different people. For some it means the accumulation of stuff: cars, furniture, and the latest electrical gadgets. For others it means security. Every extra dime is tucked away for the proverbial rainy day. To Bruce and me, money means the ability to make choices. We don't care much about cars or furniture. We lived with a decrepit old sofa for years and didn't consider replacing it until one of our hot-line kids came in, looked in the living room, and said with the complete sincerity of a six-year-old, "Oh, I'm so sorry. You must be very poor." We laughed, but we did buy some furniture after that.

However, for the most part, we just wanted to do what matters to us. To me, what matters is that I am at home. My brief adventure into full-time employment had been hard on all of us. The regular paycheck had not been worth the hassle of figuring out what to do when one of the kids got sick. I like to bake bread and clean my own house. I like to spend time in my garden and hang my sheets to dry on the clothesline.

Once we had foster children, we had priorities for them too. The best therapy is often normalizing a child. Hitting her first home run did more to bolster Lucy's self-esteem than any amount of talking. Dancing lessons and soccer camp matter to kids, but the state doesn't pay for these things. Bruce and I do. Most of our kids come to foster care suffering from the effects of a terrible diet. I think what kids eat is important, so I pay for whole grains, organic milk, and free-range eggs.

Foster children feel perpetually different. Bruce and I don't think it's healthy for them to look different. While a lot of the clothing I buy comes from consignment shops, I make sure that it's clean, appropriate, and in style. I spend more than I receive in the quarterly clothing allotment on each child, but I feel the payoff is worth it; kids who feel better about themselves do better.

Bruce and I could have lived a very different life. We could have had more time and more stuff, but I don't believe we would have been any happier. We did, and continue to do, exactly what we want. We always have a choice.

This does not mean that I am happy with the reimbursement rate that foster parents receive. I'm not. I think that to pay a family less to care for a troubled child than many people pay to board a dog is a disgrace. It's possible to raise a child on fifteen dollars a day but it shouldn't be necessary. It speaks to what we think about parents' work and children's worth.

That year, the Massachusetts State administration began a policy review to explore the possibility of increasing our reimbursement rate by a dollar a day. Meanwhile, I continued to care for Lucy and Karen and Sara and whoever else turned up on the doorstep as best I could. After one particularly tough day I called a local legislator who was most vocal in her opposition to such a raise and invited her to dinner at my home. I thought she might appreciate an opportunity to observe firsthand what life in the trenches was really like. My offer was politely but firmly declined.

A few of my close friends in the system were very politically active at this time, but in spite of how important I knew activism was, it was just not an arena that held my attention for long. I knew kids needed better services, social workers needed lighter caseloads, and foster homes needed more money, but I didn't want to write letters or call politicians or attend rallies. I just wanted to take care of my kids.

I had changed my mind about caring exclusively for sexually abused girls. I was good at it and there were an unfortunate number of them needing homes, but there was no way for me to give the level of one-on-one care that Sara required to more than one or two children at a time. Psychologically, it was terribly draining. Sara needed to process all that had happened to her, and that took time, lots of it, every day. She was compelled to tell her story to me night after night. While the frame never changed, she often added details that made what happened to her far too vivid for me. Once again, my overactive imagination turned into a considerable problem. For a while, I was plagued by disturbing nightmares about rooms full of filthy, crying babies. In these dreams, I knew I was supposed to be caring for them, but the refrigerator was empty and I couldn't find any water. Had it not been for the emotional support I received from Sara's therapist, I suspect I would have burned out early in working with her. I decided that what I needed was a new foster care challenge to energize myself the way that my new work in the department did.

For some time, I had been thinking about taking medically needy babies. I knew such children were a very tough population to find homes for. Bruce and I discussed asking for an HIV-positive infant, but after a good deal of soul searching we decided against it. Our home was a busy place with lots of little children harboring all sorts of viruses running in and out all day, and I wasn't sure I could keep a fragile infant isolated enough. And while we were both pretty well put-together adults who could handle a high level of grief and loss as well as anyone could expect, our younger kids were not, and it felt wrong to expose them to it. So we waited, knowing that the right kid would come along, and on a frigid October morning she did.

Chapter

Nine

Every new arrival is an unprecedented event, simply because each child is so unique. Case records sometimes seem to blend together in a kind of numbing sameness, but each child is uncharted territory.

When home finding or hot line calls with a placement for us, there is usually little time to give much thought to details. The immediacy of the child in the police station, the emergency room, the office, or the backseat of the worker's car is all that matters. I act first and react later when I am anesthetized somewhat by time and distance.

It was harder when I was told about Shamika. There was no child to hold or feed or bathe. Shamika lay in a hospital bed, two hundred miles away, waiting for a home to be discharged to. I knew there was something special about her: Susan, my home finder, made a special trip out to talk in person about whether we might be interested.

Susan often seemed embarrassed by what she asked of her homes, torn between the desire to protect us from what she knew would be gut-wrenching work and the necessity of finding homes for children. She seemed uncomfortable now. She twirled her teacup and tapped her pen; her eyes never quite met mine. I know now that she was trying to sanitize Shamika's story. If she kept it clinical, perhaps it wouldn't be so hard. But Susan was a mother before she was a social worker. I heard the question she couldn't ask. I was asking it myself but never voiced it out loud. How do you burn your own baby? What kind of a monster does that to a child? My questions were about scarring and medical follow-up and when we might be able to visit. I swallowed back rage with tea and muffins and small talk.

And of course, I said yes. We would be glad to have Shamika. Bruce had some vacation time coming. We could go to the hospital together to learn how to take care of her.

We had three days before her worker, Robert, was able to spare a day to go with us. I used the time to scour secondhand shops for soft old cotton and flannel clothing. Bruce got out the crib we had packed away when Karen graduated to a big bed. I bought a new mattress. It was all busywork, but it kept me occupied until I could get to her.

I was uncertain about how to present Shamika to the younger children. Her burns extended along one arm, down her chest and stomach, and across both thighs. Even with skin grafts, the scarring would stand out in rough pink relief against her brown skin. I decided to make use of Shamika's mother's story. Juanita said that her child, not yet walking, had pulled a cup of coffee off a low table. There was no need to add that the burn specialist said it could not have happened that way, that it took far more than a cup of coffee to do that much damage.

Whatever the real story, what happened next is in the record. Shamika was transported to a local hospital by ambulance. She was stabilized and then transported to a large teaching hospital with a pediatric burn unit, where she spent the next six weeks fighting off infections and receiving skin grafts on the worst burns on her stomach and legs.

There is something about entering any highly secure area that makes me feel vaguely guilty. I stutter and stammer and give far more information than I'm asked for in the vain hope that I won't look like I just walked off a locked ward someplace. Fortunately, Bruce knows how I behave and usually takes over with airport and hospital security. My nervousness about going to meet Shamika for the first time made me more nervous than ever. Robert was still looking for a parking space, and I had no idea about how to respond to questions at the front desk about whether or not we were immediate family. I was tempted to wax philosophical about our relationship as foster parents to someone who clearly didn't care, but Bruce rescued me. He just said yes, grabbed two passes, and took me to the elevator. Robert had been here a couple of times already and knew the drill. He was able to flash some official-looking identification and was issued a pass without a second look.

Even now, with the perspective of a half-dozen years behind me, I have trouble writing about Juanita. I wonder if my memory of our first meeting is still colored by the intense dislike I felt for her then. I know I was angry that I had to meet her at all. When I agreed to take Shamika I hadn't even asked about her mother. I assumed she was in jail or, at the very least, barred from contact with her daughter. It infuriated me to find out that from the very first moment, Juanita had taken full advantage of the hospital's rooming-in program. Perhaps she assumed that everyone bought her story about the burns. She had, in fact, learned only a few hours before our arrival that Shamika was going home with Bruce and me. Her presence at the hospital certainly complicated things for us.

With open hostility, Juanita watched me walk through the door. Our eyes met and held for just seconds before she turned to the crib to fuss over Shamika, talking to her in the phony, high-pitched tone of someone unused to conversing with children but wishing to convince an unappreciative audience otherwise.

I hoped the harsh overhead lighting was more flattering to me than it was to Juanita. Her medium-brown skin looked nearly yellow under the glare and still bore the traces of adolescent acne. Her hair was dry and stiff, probably the result of too many chemical attempts to change the color or curl. She was too heavy for her leopard-print leggings and fuchsia tank top, and only her nails, half-inch-long talons with carefully painted butterflies on each tip, looked clean and well tended.

I suspect that Juanita was as critical of my appearance as I was of hers. My long braid, round glasses, mid-calf corduroy skirt, and shapeless sweater must have made me appear dowdy and old-fashioned. We lived in different worlds, but we would have to find some common ground if we were ever going to work together to do the right thing for Shamika.

Robert, bless him, must have felt the tension. He casually put a hand on Juanita's shoulder and asked to speak to her in the hallway. She rolled her eyes but followed him out of the room.

I scooted over to the crib, anxious to finally meet Shamika. She wasn't what could be called a pretty baby, although not because there was anything amiss with her features. It was her demeanor that was wrong. Her deep chocolate-brown eyes lacked the spark that would have made her attractive. Shamika sat in her crib, a depressed little pot-bellied Buddha halfheartedly fingering some plastic beads.

I thought about what the first year of this child's life had been like. According to the investigator's report, Shamika bounced from place to place, bed to bed, person to person, depending on the whim of her mother, with no way to predict what the next day or even hour would bring. It was unlikely that the burns that put her in the hospital were the first or only instance of abuse she had suffered. Movement, pain, and multiple caregivers marked even her stay in the hospital. What must this baby have thought about the world?

There were no tubes or wires connecting Shamika to anything. After talking to her for a moment, I scooped her up, mindful of the wounds on her stomach. Bruce stood behind her. He reached his hand up and softly rubbed her cheek. She turned toward him, grabbing his finger and poking it into her mouth. He chuckled, pulled it out, and touched the tip of her nose. A tiny smile flashed across her face, not quite reaching those solemn little eyes, but it was enough. Bruce and I looked at each other over Shamika's curls. There were no more questions. We could love this baby.

Robert and Juanita returned from the hallway. She lost no time in snatching Shamika from me. "It's her nap time. You shouldn't have gone picking her up. Now she won't want to lie back down."

I answered in my sweetest voice. "Do you mind if I watch how you do it? Then I can follow the same routine while she's with me, so she'll feel more comfortable."

Juanita looked at me suspiciously. She wasn't buying my act for a moment. She plopped Shamika back in her crib. "Hush now. Stop your fussin'. You got no reason to be whining. Now be quiet and go to sleep." Juanita gave me an insolent stare. "I don't go for spoiling babies. You get her spoiled with you, and then I got to deal with her at home. I don't want you rocking her to sleep. I don't got time for that stuff."

I did a slow burn, but Bruce put his hand on my shoulder and I managed to keep my mouth shut. There was no point in telling Juanita that I didn't view rocking a baby as spoiling. And if it was, what could I say? My plan was to get Shamika home with us and commence spoiling her as quickly as possible.

But I could see a problem brewing, and it was likely to be a big one. I knew that my feelings toward Juanita were likely to soften with time. No doubt, her own history was as filled with neglect and abuse as Shamika's was. But that didn't change the fact that I felt she was completely incapable of caring for a child. What I really believed was that Shamika should be placed with a family who was prepared to adopt her as quickly as possible, but that was not the way the system worked. For all the talk about speeding up the adoption process for kids who were the victims of extreme abuse, the reality hadn't really changed much. It still took a couple of years to get a kid through the system. Two years might not seem long when you're forty, but it's most of your life when you're three.

Court battles and legal wrangling would rob Shamika of her childhood. She would be yet another baby sentenced to the prison of foster care for a crime she never committed. By agreeing to be her foster parents for those years, weren't Bruce and I somehow accomplices, just as guilty as everyone else? This was a question I grappled with every day and never resolved. However, in spite of any blame we might reasonably share, Shamika still needed a place to live and a family, however temporary, to care for her. We would deal with attachment issues later. Right now, we had a job to do. Part of that job was keeping a space in Shamika's world for Juanita. No matter how I felt about it, she was going to be a piece of the puzzle of Shamika's life forever.

Bruce and I spent the next two hours learning about skin grafts and burn care. It wasn't all that complicated. The burns were well healed. The scars needed to be kept clean and massaged several times a day with a gooey ointment, but that was about it. Our real job was going to be lifting Shamika out of a depression that was potentially more damaging than her physical injuries.

We left Shamika reluctantly, although we were all anxious to leave the city before rush-hour traffic. We decided on the trip home that, since Juanita had barely spoken to us the entire day, it would be best if we let Robert pick Shamika up from the hospital and bring her to us. We all wanted to avoid the scene that might erupt if Juanita was expected to hand her daughter over to us.

It was a relief when Friday finally arrived, and I knew Shamika was on her way to us. I spent the hours catching up on some long-neglected writing projects. Karen was the only child at home when Robert's battered station wagon pulled into the driveway. He carried Shamika inside, still strapped in her car seat. I removed

Shamika's hat, careful not to wake her. Karen fingered the dark curls that sprang up from Shamika's head like tiny corkscrews.

"Dis da baby, Mama. My baby?" In Karen's world, everything was hers.

"This is Shamika," I said. "Let's let her sleep. She'll wake up soon."

Robert stayed for a cup of coffee and filled me in on appointments and visitation. Because of the pending trial, I was confident that this was one case that would be micromanaged from the top down. The department would not want to risk looking foolish in court because of any avoidable screwups. Our local newspaper loved to latch on to things like that.

Robert had a word of warning before he walked out the door. "I have only referred to you by your first names, and Juanita has no idea where you live," he said. " I want to keep it that way. This family is a tough bunch with a lot of violence in their history. I think you're perfectly safe, but I still want you to keep a very low profile here. You'll probably end up testifying in court, and I don't want to put you at risk."

I hadn't ever really focused on foster parenting as a high-risk kind of job. Though there was always an element of, if not exactly danger, certainly unease about dealing with families with long criminal and psychiatric histories, I had never felt unsafe before. But Robert was right. There was a look in Juanita's eyes that I didn't like. I was not anxious to cross her. This was one of those moments when I wished one of the politicians who thought that at fifteen dollars a day I was being overpaid was around.

With Robert gone, I was free to indulge in my familiar round of "what have I gotten myself into" crazies. Finally, the older children came home, and I was able to calm down. They showed me exactly what Shamika needed.

While I fluttered around anxiously checking and rechecking my list of supplies and instructions, Shamika slumped on a play mat, not engaged in any of the brightly colored toys that surrounded her. But when Karen sat next to her and began playing with the busy box she had only recently outgrown, Shamika's eyes lit up. She put out a tentative finger then jerked it back in surprised delight when Mickey Mouse unexpectedly popped up. Within minutes, I could hear Karen's infectious giggle followed by baby babble from Shamika. The two little girls were rolling around on the carpet like a couple of pudgy puppies. I finally relaxed. Shamika wasn't going to break. After all, she was just a baby, and she needed the same things any other baby might need. Mostly, she needed someone to pay attention to her.

I had warned the children to approach Shamika quietly. I feared she was so depressed that she could be easily overwhelmed. For a change, they came in quietly rather than sounding like the invasion of Normandy. Shamika was a bit shy at first, hiding her head in my shoulder when they came too close. But she warmed up in a few minutes, not exactly joining in but certainly interested as long as she could keep me in her line of sight. This was one of those little miracles that I never tired of. How do they know? What instinct kicks in that tells these children who the mother is? I have seen it too often for it to be a coincidence. In a room full of unfamiliar adults, babies just coming into care unfailingly gravitate toward the foster mother.

Only Sara remained unmoved. Sara was far too fragile to tolerate the intrusion of yet another needy child. When she voiced her considerable displeasure (well, not voiced exactly—she peeled a large section of paper from the kitchen wall and I got the message), I had to acknowledge that she had a point. Sara needed, and should have had, a home where the focus would be entirely on her. But so did all my other children. The nature of the foster care beast is that the very children least equipped to deal with the busy, chaotic, and unpredictable world of a foster home have no other option. Lots of children and a limited pool of foster families virtually assure a foster child of a life of not quite enough time, energy, or attention. I loved what I was doing, but I didn't love its limitations. I often vowed to cut back on my numbers, but I never followed through. There was always another call, another child, another story. In the end, we all lost something.

But we adapted too. I know that I developed more tolerance and flexibility than I otherwise would have. I had to hope that all the children came out of the experience having gained something from all the loss.

Our first week with Shamika passed, then the second and the third, and before we knew when or could begin to explain how, Shamika became one of us. Each day there was a change in her. She had lost a lot of ground while in the hospital, and there was a lot of catching up for her to do. It seemed that one day she could barely crawl and the next I was pulling her off the middle of the dining room table. She came with no speech and was soon picking up a word or two a day. Almost overnight, Shamika transformed from a solemn little waif into a ham. When she discovered she could make us laugh with her antics, she was unstoppable. I wondered how I had ever found her plain.

There was no way for us to know how the criminal case against

Juanita was going. Periodically, people from the district attorney's office would call with a question about something, but they never offered any information. I saw Robert every couple of weeks when he picked Shamika up for her visit, but he didn't know much about that piece of it either. If past history were any example, it would likely be months before the case came to trial and months, if not years, longer before the appeals were exhausted and a decision arrived at. Until that was resolved there was no way the department was going to do anything about changing the goal for Shamika to adoption. I expected that Shamika would be with us for a long, long time. Long enough for us to love her. Long enough for her to love us. Long enough to cross the line to forever.

I never figured out how I was supposed to do it. How was I supposed to give enough to each of these kids to let them grow up with the sense of family they needed to be healthy without loving them too much to let them go in the end? In my heart, Karen was already my child. Lucy and Angie were for all intents and purposes sisters. Sara would never make it anyplace but with us. I still worried and fretted over Danny's fate. It is the triumph of foster care that families can love these children who were never meant to be theirs. It is also the tragedy.

Mid-December approached. On one of those dull Saturdays that could only be further dulled by a trip to the mall, Bruce and I decided to finish up the Christmas shopping. My plan to have everything bought and wrapped by Thanksgiving had gone the way of most of my other good intentions, and now I was scrambling. In an effort to prevent total bedlam at home, we elected to take Sara, Karen, and Shamika with us. The older kids could manage nicely without us for a few hours.

We had just pulled into the mall's overflowing parking garage when Bruce's beeper began its annoying chirp. This device was the bane of my existence, but, given the number of hot-line calls we received at inopportune moments, I usually didn't complain about his on-call status at work.

"I don't suppose you can ignore it," I said hopefully.

"I better not. It's from home."

My stomach gave a quick lurch. I knew the kids would never beep us for anything short of a real emergency. After a frustrating search we located a phone booth. I sat in the car with the children while Bruce called home, biting my nails and making deals with God.

Bruce was back in a couple of minutes. He actually left a slight trail of rubber leaving the parking lot.

"Just tell me," I said.

"Who's Monica Feldman?" he asked in reply.

"The social services area program manager. Why?"

"She just called Nathan. Seems that Shamika's father was released from prison a few weeks ago. The police got word from Juanita's sister that he found out where his kid is and he's planning to get her. The police called the DA and the DA called DSS."

I dropped my head into my hands.

"Apparently he can be violent, but they don't think he has a gun."

For an instant I thought I might faint. Bruce patted my leg.

"The local police are already at our house, and the state police are on their way. The boys called their friends, and half the neighborhood is there for reinforcements. The kids are fine, Kathy." Bruce meant to reassure me, but I noticed that he was not exactly following the posted speed limit in his rush to get home.

Thank goodness Nathan had reached us. If I had arrived home unprepared for the sight of a yard full of flashing lights and squad cars it might have been the end of me. A uniformed officer met us at the car and insisted on carrying Shamika into the house. I was grateful that she was fast asleep. She had had enough of sirens and lights in her short life.

We had barely removed our coats when two hot-line workers I knew only slightly showed up to take Shamika. "Wait a minute," protested Bruce. "Let's think about this for a minute. The only report we have that Shamika's father knows where she is and is planning to get her is coming from Juanita's sister. She's not the most credible person in the world, and she hates the guy. Realistically, what are the chances that he wants a baby he's only seen twice badly enough to risk jail time? Even if he did, how could he have found us? Besides, if he's really going to try to get her, he'll try whether you move her or not. Couldn't we at least wait until Monday and see how things look then?"

The workers looked at each other. Bruce must have felt them softening.

"Look," he continued. "This kid has been through a lot. She's just starting to settle in. If you move her again with no preparation she may not recover. Please. Can't you talk to somebody? I promise. Nobody is going to touch this baby."

One worker spoke up. "The call isn't mine. But I'll talk to Monica. She was pretty determined to get this kid out of here today."

"Use the phone in the kitchen," Bruce replied.

Bruce next talked to the police, who talked to social services, who talked again to Bruce. I was glad for the reprieve. I needed to calm down the other kids. Karen was fine, and I think Neddy and

Ben were rather enjoying the drama, but Lucy, Angie, and Sara were a mess. Memories of police in their own living rooms were still too raw for them. We sat together tightly on the sofa while the chaos swirled around us.

Too soon, the adults gathered again. "Here's the deal," the first worker began. "The area program manager has agreed to let Shamika stay here. They'll conference first thing Monday morning and decide what to do next. If there's any trouble, we'll be here within thirty minutes to pick her up. The police will drive by every hour or so to check things out. If you call nine-eleven, they'll have someone here in less than five minutes. We had to do a lot of fancy talking to get the higher-ups to agree to this; I sure hope nothing goes wrong."

"Nothing will go wrong," Bruce promised.

For the rest of the evening, the middle kids kept themselves busy booby-trapping doors and developing elaborate spy plans. Maybe I should have stopped them, but I preferred to see them feeling powerful and in control rather than quaking in fear.

The night was uneventful, although we adults did not sleep very well. I kept Shamika in the small crib next to my bed, and I awoke with every small noise she made.

By Sunday afternoon we were breathing a bit easier. I figured this for one of those moments that would go down in family history and be remembered with a shudder and a smile.

The call came at three o'clock.

"Hello, Kathy? It's Monica Feldman. I'm sorry to bother you, but there has been a change in plans. I've spent the better part of the afternoon talking with the assistant DA and my regional supervisor. They think I was a bit hasty in allowing Shamika to stay with you last night. If there is any chance that there has been a breach of confidentiality on this case, well, we just can't take the risk. I know you understand. The hot-line team is on the way now. We appreciate your willingness to hang in, but we can't afford to take any chances."

I ranted and raved, but in the end I had no choice. I packed a bag with Shamika's things and wrote a detailed letter about her skin care and her appointments. I didn't write about who she was or what it felt like to be her mother. That would be for her next foster mother to discover.

The kids had a hard time saying good-bye. I knew the boys would be fine, but I worried about the others. They acted out in the ways their histories had taught them, Sara with rage and Angie with withdrawal, but underneath were the same familiar feelings of loss and fear.

Chapter

Ten

When my boys were little, I measured time by their milestones: first steps, first words, first day of school. The predictability of their development defined my life as surely as the emergence of spring after the snows of winter defined the seasons. Now that our sons were nearly grown and our daughters not far behind, the way I measured time had changed. As a foster parent, I was well aware that I might not be in a child's life long enough to see her learn to ride a bike or jump from Brownie to Girl Scout. I had learned to be satisfied with smaller snippets of time and milestones that were not so easily recognized. I wasn't there to celebrate Sara's first tooth, but we had ice cream to mark her first week without a trip to the principal for swearing at somebody.

I measured the time a foster child was with us not from birthday to birthday but from case review to case review. Every six months, all of the people involved in a foster child's life are invited to the social services office to discuss what is happening with his or her family and to look at the progress made on the child's service plan. A service plan outlines the tasks that everyone—social services, foster parents, and birth family—is required to complete before a child can return home.

There are more people involved in these meetings than one might think. In addition to birth parents, foster parents, social workers, and attorneys, there are usually people referred to as "collaterals" present. These are the outside service providers like therapists, court-appointed guardians, probation officers, and school personnel. Meetings are led by a social worker who is otherwise not involved with the case. He or she is assisted by a community volunteer who is there to add another layer of oversight. If there was more than one child in care, and that was true more often than not, there would be multiples of all these folks. I have been to case reviews with twenty people in the room, all of whom want to have their say. At the end of the meeting, the case reviewer will determine who is in compliance with his tasks and who is not. If the birth parents are in compliance, a date for the children to be returned home is set. If they have not done what is required of them, the goal might be changed to adoption.

Complicated though this process might seem, it serves a useful purpose. Prior to the initiation of the case review system in the mid-eighties, children in care sometimes got lost (and sometimes still do). I mean that in the literal sense. A new worker might have gone to visit a child from a case he had just received only to find the kid had been moved and no one was sure where to. Until then, there was no real system for tracking a child in care. Kids often just drifted around with no plan to fix the family problems that landed them in care or to find a permanent home for them if they were unable to return home. The case review process was developed to make sure that this would no longer happen. It wasn't a perfect solution—kids still spent too long without a permanency plan—but it made things a lot better. At least one knew that, twice a year, someone was going to be looking in on a kid. It kept people on their toes.

I went faithfully to the reviews for Karen, Lucy, and Sara. They were difficult for me to sit through because nothing ever changed for these kids. Karen's goal was still adoption, but no adoption worker had been assigned to her. These assignments happen on a first come, first served basis. In the meantime, Bonnie was doing better. She was in a family shelter and had been sober for several weeks. My biggest fear was that Bonnie would do well enough to convince those involved in her case to change the goal for Karen back to reunification before an adoption worker was assigned. While I could accept that this was the way the system was supposed to work—parents were supposed to get their lives in order and get their children back—I could hardly imagine losing Karen.

Lucy was on hold as well. One case review, then another, was held. Both times I was told that a worker would be assigned any day. But while Lucy waited for a worker, her life was getting lived. She learned how to make fudge and catch a pop fly. She grew taller, older, "less desirable" than a younger child, and more attached to us.

Karen and Lucy were in better shape than Sara. At least with a change in goal to adoption, they were on the road to some sort of resolution about their futures. But until Sara was stable enough to testify against her father, she couldn't even get that far. Her stated goal was still family stabilization and reunification, even though there was no family to stabilize or reunify. No one had heard from Sharon for months, and Sara's father hadn't seen any of his children for even longer. They all refused to visit him.

The children were scattered: Sara's sister was still in a psychiatric hospital, and her brother was bouncing through his fourth foster placement. But these were the rules. No move could be made toward permanency for at least a year, then we'd all have to wait for an adoption worker, wait for an adoptive family, wait for a trial, wait for an appeal. Years would likely go by before Sara could hope for a family to call her own. It wasn't fair to anyone.

I started to make phone calls, going a bit higher and getting a bit angrier with each one. Shortly after Christmas, I got a call from the adoption supervisor telling me that Karen and Lucy had both been assigned a worker. Karen was actually further down on the list and should have had to wait longer, but with both children in the same house, it seemed prudent to assign them together. It seemed like a remarkably sensible idea from a department that was seldom remarkably sensible.

Karen's social worker had pretty much dropped out of the picture at the same time Lucy's had. As far as I was concerned, she had never been very diligent anyway. It seemed to me that she usually did the absolute minimum and was content to let me do as much of the work involved with transportation and visitation as I liked. Once the goal was changed to adoption for the girls, it seemed to me that both of their workers felt that their jobs were done. They just appeared to be killing time until the case officially came off their roles.

I took Karen to the shelter each week to see Bonnie. A social worker from that program supervised the one-hour visit while I found something to do. The visits remained nightmares. Karen had huge problems with separation. I called Linda a few times to ask if she had any advice about how I might handle the problem, but when she didn't return my calls, I decided to take matters into my own hands. I called Bonnie and asked if we could talk. She was willing, if not exactly anxious, and we met the next day.

"Look," I began. "I know we haven't been the best of friends, but we both love Karen. These visits aren't getting any easier for her, so here was what I was thinking . . ."

"I'm not giving up my visits," she interrupted. "I still want my daughter back. I'm doing better now, and my lawyer thinks I've got a good chance."

"I wasn't asking for that. You're right. Karen could go back to you, and you need to visit." I paused, then continued. "But maybe for the next few visits the three of us could do something together. Just go to lunch or something. I think if Karen sees the two of us together once in a while she might not get so scared when I leave her. If she does go home she'll need to transition back slowly. The whole thing will be easier if you and I are . . . well . . . friends."

Bonnie was quiet for a minute. "I've been thinking the same thing actually. I know she loves you. I was thinking it might be better for her if she still got to see you."

"How about tomorrow? Would you like to go to Friendly's? It's Karen's favorite restaurant. Actually, any place with ice cream is Karen's favorite restaurant."

Bonnie managed a small smile. "I'm an ice cream freak too."

So the new visits began. They were a bit awkward at first. Karen called me Mommy, and, even though I referred to Bonnie as

Mommy in front of her, she never called Bonnie anything at all. But she did warm up to Bonnie pretty quickly, giving me some pangs when I saw the two of them together. There could be no mistaking their relationship; they looked so much alike. On our second visit, I brought along pictures of Bruce and the children. I had some great shots of all of us camping and on Christmas ski trips. Bonnie spent a lot of time pouring over the pictures and had question after question.

"Who's this? Your mom or your husband's? Do all of you ski? Which one plays the flute?" And finally, "How many kids do you have? I didn't know you had already adopted some."

The next week Bonnie had a memento of her own to share. She brought Karen her childhood bear. "It's the only happy thing I remember from when I was little," she told me wistfully. "I used to hold him and hide under my bed when my parents fought. I want Karen to have him." We were quiet for a moment.

I finally broke the silence. "Karen seems pretty comfortable with you now. Next time, do you want to see her alone?"

"Okay," Bonnie replied. "You know, I'm not a bad person. I've done some things I shouldn't have. I've made really bad choices. Except for when I was at Sanctuary House and now here, I've never been really clean since I was fourteen. It's funny because I always said I would never drink. I hated it. I don't remember the last time I saw my stepmother sober. My dad was a drunk too. He killed himself when I was thirteen."

There wasn't anything I could say.

"I would do better by Karen. I wouldn't let her grow up like I did."

"I know, Bonnie. I know you love her. I know you wouldn't do anything on purpose to hurt her."

· · ·

Bonnie looked awful when I brought Karen to her the next Saturday. Always slender, she looked emaciated, with purple smudges under both eyes. Her skin was pasty gray, and her hands shook when she unfastened Karen's car seat.

"Are you up for this?" I asked. "You don't look like you feel very well."

"I'm okay. Just a little tired. I really want to see her."

Karen looked solemn when I drove off, but for the first time, she didn't cry. I was torn between happiness that she was finally adjusting and jealousy when I saw her slip her hand into Bonnie's. The hour crawled by. I tried to do some shopping, but I couldn't find anything that interested me. My mind was back at the shelter, wrapped around Karen and Bonnie.

I returned fifteen minutes earlier than I should have. A staff member answered the front doorbell and brought me into the communal living room.

Bonnie was slipping Karen into her coat. There were two large boxes on the floor next to her. As soon as Karen caught my eye she pulled away from Bonnie and ran to me.

"Wanna see my doll, Mommy? I got a new doll."

Bonnie looked even worse than when I saw her earlier. She had been crying. Like me, Bonnie was not a pretty crier. Her face was a mass of red blotches and her eyes were swollen. "Can you wait a minute?" she asked. "I want to give you some stuff for Karen, and I need to talk to you."

Together we wrestled two boxes out to my van, with Karen

walking behind me, unwilling to let go of my coattail. When we finally got boxes and baby loaded in I turned toward Bonnie. She was
leaning against the door of the van, crying softly into her hands.

"I'm signing the surrender," she said.

"Why?" I asked, genuinely puzzled.

"I don't know. The pictures I guess. You look like the kind of
family I wish I had."

"We're not perfect," I told her. "We argue. I don't always have
enough time for everybody. Lots of times my kids probably wish
they had better parents than they do. I don't want you to decide to
give Karen up because you think I'm somebody I'm not.

"Well, I can't fight to keep her thinking I'm somebody I'm not
either. I'm sober today, but I may not be next week or even tomorrow. I can't give her what you can."

I started to interrupt, but she waved her hand to stop me. "I'm
not talking about the stuff," she said. "I mean, I'm glad she'll have
the music lessons and the sports with you, but that's not what I'm
talking about. I'm talking about the guarantees. That you'll be
there for her. She'll never go to sleep and wonder what she's going
to wake up to. She can bring her friends home. She'll have a life
and a family, her family. With me, who knows?"

I had hated Bonnie. I had felt anger and pity and jealousy, all of
the emotions you might expect, given our odd history. I never expected to feel what I felt now, which was awe. I was humbled by
her courage and selflessness.

"The stuff in the boxes—it'll be too big now," she said. "When
you give it to her, later, would you tell her it's from me?"

"You can tell her. You can still see her."

"No I can't. I'm not that strong. I can't give her up if I have to see her. Don't bring her back."

I pulled Bonnie into my arms like I had pulled so many other hurt children. Right now, that's what she was. I wondered what her life would have been like if she had found a safe haven at thirteen. When I looked at Karen snuggling her baby doll in the backseat, I had a pretty good idea.

By the time I got home, I was able to put my sympathy for Bonnie's grief aside and revel in the moment. Karen would be ours! No more worry or sleepless nights thinking about making a life without her. Bruce and I could hardly believe it. The trial we dreaded would never need to happen.

I was on the phone to Karen's worker at nine o'clock on Monday morning to give her the rundown on what had happened on Saturday. Shockingly, she was in the office and taking calls. "So all you need to do," I finished up, "is get Bonnie into the office to sign the papers and it's a done deal."

"Sounds good," Linda said. "I'll get to it right away. I'm sure she'll want her attorney there, but that won't be a problem. We could have it wrapped up by Friday. The adoption worker, Meg Richards, just got the record last week. So the case isn't really mine, but I should probably set up the meeting anyway since Bonnie's never met Meg."

I waited until Friday, then left a message for Linda. I called back the following week. No, Linda hadn't set up the meeting. She'd been busy. By the end of the week for sure. The next Friday came and went with no meeting and no signature. But Linda's calendar wasn't too bad after Monday. She would see to it then. I left messages but got no return call. The following Monday she called to say she'd set up the termination meeting with Bonnie, only to find that Bonnie had packed her things and signed herself out of the program five days earlier. She'd left no forwarding address, and no one at the shelter had heard from her. She was just gone, without a trace and without signing the surrender.

Chapter

Eleven

❖

I was furious both at Linda and her attitude, which seemed far too cavalier, given that Karen's future was back on hold.

"Don't worry," Linda said. "Either she'll show up and we'll get the surrender, or she won't and we'll get the termination on grounds of desertion. It may take a while but . . ."

It was galling because it didn't need to have happened. Linda knew how fragile Bonnie was. In my view, that surrender should have been her first priority. The only bright spot was that the case was transferred to the adoption worker. Meg Richardson was a terrific social worker. I knew her from the hot line and couldn't think of anyone I would rather have worked with. Though her degree was not in social work but in education, anything she may have lacked in course work she more than made up for in common sense and people skills.

Because Meg was assigned to two children who lived in my house, Lucy and Karen, she had to figure out a way to draw professional boundaries between the two cases. It would take some extraordinary juggling to make sure that each child's needs remained separate. First, Meg met with Bruce and me to get to know us as Karen's prospective parents. Later, she met with Karen. Meg then met once again with Bruce and me and made it clear she was there to talk only about Lucy, who she was and what might be best for her in terms of a family. From her perspective, Karen's case might take some time, but the outcome was not in much doubt—low legal risk was how she put it. Lucy's case carried more risk but not enough to delay finding a family for her.

"Actually, Meg," I said, during that get-to-know-you visit, "Bruce and I were thinking it might be better if you just left Lucy with us. She's happy here, and she's doing pretty well in school. And I think Ellen might sign a surrender if she could see Lucy once in a while."

Meg looked at Bruce and me. When she spoke, it was clear where she stood. This was one worker who would never take the easy way out at the expense of a kid.

"How do you feel about Karen?"

"I'm not sure what you're asking. Karen is our daughter. We couldn't love her more had she been born to us. When I think about our family, I have six kids. The birth status isn't really an issue. Why?"

"What about Lucy? Do you feel the same about her?"

I squirmed around, suddenly uncomfortable in my seat.

"Well, no. I suppose I don't. I can't speak for Bruce, of course, but for myself, well, I care about her. She's really a great kid. It isn't the same as with the other kids, but I think I could grow to love her."

Bruce agreed. "I'm probably more connected to her than Kathy is, but I know what she means. Lucy doesn't feel like she's ours the way the other kids do."

"Don't you think that Lucy deserves better than a family who likes her? Why shouldn't she get what Karen has, a family who thinks the sun rises and sets with her? Sorry, guys. You're nice people, but you're not the family for Lucy."

We were a bit embarrassed but relieved. Meg was right: We cared about Lucy, but neither one of us really wanted seven kids. Lucy was a terrific kid who deserved more than to be adopted out of pity. Still, once again I grappled with the sense of not being good enough to do this work. I so wanted to be a saint, the good guy in the white hat, the cavalry riding to the rescue, and I had to settle for just being human.

Meg met several times alone with Lucy, who had a tough time with those visits. She certainly enjoyed the one-on-one attention she got from Meg, but her loyalty toward her mother was so strong that she always felt guilty for having so much fun. Then there was the problem of discussing the kind of family she wanted. Lucy didn't care about whether or not she would be an only child or have several brothers and sisters. What she really wanted was to go home to Ellen. She wanted her mom to grow up.

Late in January, Meg came by again, this time with a camcorder. She took an hour's worth of video of Lucy. She caught her in the yard building a snowman, playing dress-up with Sara, and reading to Karen. She played talk-show host and interviewed Lucy about school and sports. Afterward, she had me fill out a questionnaire about Lucy. Other than her weak academics, there wasn't much negative to say. Lucy was a walking example of something I was to hear a lot about in the next few years—resilience.

Lucy wasn't a showy kid. She wasn't beautiful or brilliant, but she didn't need to be the center of attention. She was content to do the right thing and take pleasure where she could find it. She was grateful for a sunny day or a rainy one, for new jeans or a second-hand dress, for a home run or a C in spelling. She didn't have a mean bone in her body. Some family was going to be very lucky.

Two weeks went by before I heard from Meg again. She asked if she could come by that Friday and see Lucy, preferably without the other kids around. Easier said than done, I thought. Finding privacy at our house was never easy. I could turn off the phone, but, with at least one of the older kids out and Bruce on call at work, I didn't like to do that. All of the kids got antsy if my attention was turned elsewhere for too long, but Sara turned into a complete maniac. She had a number of troubling behaviors on a good day, and she was so overstimulated that sometimes the only safe place for her was wrapped securely in my arms. On a bad day, she was incorrigible. Having a social worker visit was always a very bad day for Sara. This was particularly true since her own worker, a woman she had only begun to trust, had just left the agency for a new job.

I finally decided to pay Neddy to keep Karen and Sara occupied upstairs. It was asking for trouble, but I really didn't have a choice.

Meg arrived right on time (another miracle for a social worker). She had a large photo album in her arms which she set carefully to one side. After some small talk she got to the point of her visit.

"Do you know," she said to Lucy, "that I have the best job in the whole world? I get to find families for children. Now, I know that you already have two families. You have a birth mother, Ellen, who will always care about you and you will always care about her. But you can't live together. Your mom has a lot of problems that make it too hard for her to take care of you and keep you safe. That's why you came to Bruce and Kathy's house. They're your family too. But a foster family is a for-a-while family. It's a place to live while your mom and your social worker and your lawyer and a judge figure out what's best for you. Bruce and Kathy care about you and you care about them, but this isn't the family you need to grow up in. You need a special family just for you. That's why I'm here. My job is to find that special family. And I think I may have done it."

Lucy's eyes filled with tears, and her bottom lip trembled. Meg pulled the album to her lap.

"This is a book that this family made just for you. Let's look at it together."

I was sitting across the room, unsure if I was included in the invitation. When Lucy didn't move, I got up and took her by the hand.

"Come on. Let's look together," I said.

Lucy scooted a bit closer to Meg and kept hold of my hand.

The scrapbook was wonderful. There were pages devoted to the family (mom, dad, and a grown-up son), one to the extended family (grandparents, aunts, uncles, and what appeared to be several dozen cousins), and even a page for the family dog. There were vacation pictures and school pictures and house and neighborhood pictures. Each page had written explanations and comments that were warm and welcoming. The final page was a picture of the room that Sam and Edith Malloy had done over for Lucy. It was a dream of a room—pink, with stenciled roses and a matching pink and white comforter and curtains. The bookcase was full, and an ornate dollhouse filled one corner. By the time she had finished taking in each picture, Lucy was looking a lot more enthusiastic. She even had some questions.

"Would I be the only kid? Do I have to call them Mom and Dad? Did they really pick me out?"

Meg answered each question honestly.

"Yep. Their son is already grown up. And, yes, they did pick you out from all the other children they heard about." Talking about what to call them was harder. "You won't have to call them Mom and Dad right away. We'll take our time. First, you can meet them here. After a day or two, they'll come by and take you out for a while. Maybe the next day, you can go to their house for dinner. After that, you'll have a few overnights, and then we'll talk about when you can move in. Once you live together for a while, you'll probably want to call them Mom and Dad. You'll feel like that's who they are."

"But what about my real mom? She won't like it if I call somebody else mom."

"Adoption isn't like foster care, Lucy. Foster care is only for a while, and you don't need to call your foster parents mom and dad unless you want to. Adoption is different. Adoption means this is a new family. It means 'These people are my mother and my father because they love me and take care of me.' That doesn't mean that you'll stop caring about Ellen and she'll stop loving you. You'll still see each other once in a while, and when you grow up you may want to see her more. But for now, Sam and Edith will be your real parents, your family."

"What if I don't like them? Do I still have to go?"

"I picked out a family that you will like," Meg answered. "There won't be an adoption until you feel ready."

I broke in next. "When can we meet them?"

"I thought Lucy might like to skip school on Thursday morning and have them drop by here."

That only gave me two days to get Lucy ready. I so wanted her to feel positive about the meeting, but I knew I would have to settle for not having her scared out of her wits. I tried to imagine what this must be like for her. Suppose I was told that I had to go be the new mom in a new family? Even if my own family wasn't perfect, or even very good, wouldn't I rail against the lack of control? Would I be happy to go, or would I be angry and frightened and not at all committed to making it work? I could imagine acting so unpleasant that the new family would send me back as soon as possible.

Even being a weekend houseguest can be uncomfortable for an adult with experience and emotional resources at his disposal. Lucy was only nine and had no choice in the matter. I could only guess what she must be going through.

In an effort to help, I made up a story about a little mouse named Boo who goes to live with a family of rabbits. I can't take too much credit for how the story came out, because a good deal of it was just me asking questions and Lucy supplying the answers. In the end, we decided that Boo would always be a mouse and his family would always be rabbits, but together they were still a family who cared about and respected one another.

Edith Malloy called Wednesday evening, ostensibly to get directions, but I think that was just an excuse. She really wanted to talk about Lucy. I was impressed, both by her warmth and her commitment to make a better life for Lucy.

I gave her a lot of information that she had already heard from Meg, but I was able to attach the reality of who Lucy was to it. Edith had a lot of questions about Lucy's mom. I knew exactly how she felt. It was important to have a sense of this mother before Edith would feel good about offering a home to Lucy. None of us who adopt want to steal children from parents who are struggling with nothing except issues of poverty. We only want to give homes to children who really need them. I ended our conversation by telling Edith about Lucy's birthday. I told her about the gift of boy clothes to a child who longed for something pretty, something yellow. Edith was quiet, absorbing this piece of Lucy.

Meg arrived early on Thursday morning. She caught Lucy and me running around in a frantic if futile attempt to get the house and ourselves presentable before the Malloys arrived. Lucy made an attempt to downplay her interest in them, but I noticed that she put on her favorite dress, a yellow and white dotted Swiss with daisies embroidered on the bodice. It was a bit frilly for my taste and didn't really suit Lucy, but she loved the dress and always seemed to walk a bit taller in it.

Just before ten, I heard a car in the driveway. It wasn't the Malloys as I expected, but rather Bruce, whom I didn't expect at all. He had managed to slip out of work for a few hours so he could be with Lucy on such a hard and important morning. I thought it likely that he wanted a chance to meet with the new family as much as I did. He hadn't been in the house thirty seconds when the Malloys showed up. As usual, my fantasy of a quiet, serene meeting was replaced by the reality of life at the Harrisons'. Everyone was talking at once, Karen started crying, the phone rang, and our new puppy wet on the floor from all the excitement. If the Malloys were overwhelmed by the chaos, they hid it well. Edith picked up Karen. Meg grabbed the phone. Bruce attended to the puppy problem. Sam took charge of the coffee pot, and I attempted introductions.

After five minutes, it felt as though we had been friends forever. That's how the Malloys affected everyone. If my car broke down in a parking lot or I got lost in an unfamiliar city, these were the folks I would hope I could ask for help. There was nothing fancy about them. They weren't out to save the world. They were just nice people. Because they didn't try to impress us, they managed to do just that.

Edith was wearing jeans (another mark in the plus column). She sat cross-legged on the floor with her family album in her lap. She talked about each page, adding details and little stories about the people and the places. Slowly, Lucy unpeeled herself from the spot where she was wedged between Bruce and me and moved closer to Edith. Without us being really aware of how and when it happened, Lucy managed to end up next to her with Sam closing in on the other side. There was a moment when Edith caught Sam's eye over Lucy's head. Her eyes were bright with tears, and she had the sweetest smile on her face. Sam reached over and patted his wife's hand, then very gently touched Lucy's braid.

I left the room, hoping everyone would assume I was after

more coffee. Meg, of course, knew better. She caught me in the mudroom, sniveling into a dish towel. She didn't say anything. She didn't need to. Besides, she was close to tears herself.

The Malloys left soon after, with a promise to call to say good night. It was a promise they kept, as they did all the promises they made to Lucy.

Lucy went from ducking behind me when the Malloys showed up and refusing to talk to them on the phone to racing out to meet them and grabbing the phone on the first ring when she was expecting a call. Bit by bit, she began to pull away from Bruce and me as she spent more time with her new family. When I asked her what she wanted to do for her social studies project, she answered the question I hadn't yet asked.

"My mom—I mean Edith—well, you know. We're going to make a Native American village. We've already got a lot of the stuff, and Sam made a huge platform for it. They're even coming to school with me next week. I'll bet ours will be the best one. You can come too, if you want to."

Okay. So I was jealous a little. Maybe I was jealous a lot. But I was a realist too. I called Meg at the office. By the time she got back to me, I knew what I had to say.

"What are we waiting for? Long transitions are fine for little kids or for families who aren't quite jelling, but these guys are all ready. Why torture them with all the traveling when they just want to be together?"

"I was going to call you this week and suggest the same thing. Sam called on Monday, and they really want Lucy in her new school soon so she has a chance to make friends before summer. He wants to get her signed up for softball too. What do you think?

Maybe you could bring most of her stuff over there next weekend, and she could move the following weekend? That would give her a chance to say good-bye to everyone at school without feeling rushed. It will give me a chance to plan a visit with Ellen too. Have you talked to her?"

"She called a couple of times, but she didn't say much," I answered. "She's got an attorney who thinks she's being railroaded, and she seems to think it's all some huge misunderstanding. Apparently, she didn't mean it when she offered to give Lucy to Bruce and me. She was just stressed out is what she is saying now."

"I want Ellen to meet Sam and Edith, but I don't want her laying a huge guilt trip on Lucy," Meg said. "She is entitled to a visit this month. Maybe we'll get lucky and she'll blow this one off."

"I don't think so. Now that she's worried about going to court she's been a lot better about calling and showing up when she's supposed to."

"We won't be going to court until fall. No way she can keep up with being mother of the year until then. My guess is she'll be pregnant by then."

This was a terrible prediction. "What makes you say that?" I asked.

"So many of these really needy moms do it over and over," Meg replied. "They get pregnant so they'll have someone to love them. They forget that babies are big bundles of need. It doesn't take long for them to get sick of being the one to do all the giving. They neglect the baby, lose custody, and a year or two later do it all over again. I just placed a three-year-old with the family that already adopted his two older sisters, and mom is pregnant again."

On Friday, we piled as much of Lucy's stuff into the van as we could and drove an hour and a half to the Malloys'. They lived in a friendly-looking subdivision. Spring had come earlier down in the valley, and already driveways were littered with bikes and basketballs. Lucy was bouncing around in our backseat, hyper in a way that was unusual for her.

Edith met us at the door. In an amazingly short time, the van was emptied, the kitchen was full, and Lucy was pulling me down the hallway to show me her bedroom.

I stood in the doorway, unable to speak. I remembered those pictures of the beautiful pink room with the matching curtains and hand-stenciled roses, and I remembered how quiet Edith got when I told her how Lucy longed for something pretty, something yellow. Obviously, elves had gone to work in the intervening weeks because a transformation had taken place. The room was no longer pink. The curtains and bedspread were gone, all replaced by fabrics in the dazzling, sunshine colors of daffodils.

Chapter

Twelve

As fall approached, Bruce Jr. moved into his own apartment, and Nathan went off to college. Benjamin and Neddy were in high school. Sports and music kept them so busy that they seldom arrived home before seven in the evening. Angie was in junior high school and involved in several after-school activities as well. Gradually, it seemed that the focus of our family was shifting from our biological and adopted children, whom we referred to as the olders, to our younger foster children.

A lovely two-year-old named Yolanda had joined Karen and Sara in the big bedroom upstairs. Yolanda had actually lived with us for a few months the previous year. Her mother, Anya, had serious mental health issues. When she took her medication she did a good job caring for her little girl. When Anya didn't take her medication, she heard voices from the radio telling her that aliens were coming to abduct her daughter. Because Anya was refusing to be medicated, Yolanda had spent the five months before coming back to us locked in her mother's small apartment, watching television and eating. She had been plump when she arrived the first time; now she was positively obese.

Yolanda was so depressed for her first two weeks with us that we felt as though we were living with Eeyore, but as she got outside, returned to school, and began a normal pattern of eating, the bubbly personality we remembered reemerged. Before long, her infectious giggle could be heard throughout the house. Everybody loved Yolanda. Even Sara, who usually disliked anyone who competed with her for my attention, sought her out to play games with.

One unexpected perk to having Yolanda placed with us was that she and Dan now shared the same social worker. Through him, I was able to keep tabs on where Dan was and how he was doing. The news was never good. He was bouncing from program to program with no one place able to meet his multiple special needs, but at least I knew where he was. Not that my knowing was helpful to Dan. Once I was no longer his foster parent, I lost all control over his life. Still, I appreciated hearing about him and being able to fantasize that the next move would be the right one for him.

Although Karen, Sara, and Yolanda now formed the core group of children in the house, others were coming and going fairly regularly. The name of each was added to a list that I carefully keep posted on my refrigerator door, amid the flotsam and jetsam of family life: tiny fruit-shaped magnets that hold a recipe for blueberry muffins, a dental appointment reminder, and a birthday invitation. Lucy's spelling test might hang alongside Ben's soccer award letter. Then there are the notes to myself: Thursday, ten-thirty. What Thursday? Where was I supposed to be? Did I go there? Did someone come here? Periodically, I go on a cleaning spree and sort everything out. The pictures go into albums, the appointments into my master calendar. Most of it goes into the trash, no longer important enough to keep.

My list, though, never gets filed or tossed or recycled. I began keeping it when I came across a picture of a little boy one day, a cute little guy with big dark eyes and chubby cheeks whom I couldn't for the life of me identify. I had a vague recollection of taking him to church with us one morning, but I couldn't remember his name or the circumstances of his arrival. That incident bothered me for days. If a child was with me, even briefly, I needed a way to note that as a fact, as a piece of history. To forget or dismiss even one child diminished not only the child but me as well. So I began the list.

It wasn't much. Just a first name, an age (approximate), the length of stay, and maybe a detail that seemed significant. Sometimes I was able to add a destination, home, shelter, or hospital. The list gave my life a structure, a frame that I felt I needed.

One name on it, however, lacked any of the little details. It was just a first name, Audrey, and nothing else. There wasn't anything else to add; Audrey never left because she never actually arrived.

When Bruce and I found out that Lucy was definitely being adopted, we had begun to think about another long-term placement. Once again, we were interested in a medically needy baby. There is no shortage of children ill enough to need a full-time, at-home parent, and my social worker, Susan, was able to present us with two babies in less than a week. The first had been rather badly beaten; it was too soon to determine just how much care she was likely to need. The second had been injured not by her parents but by fate, and that was the child we decided to take.

Audrey had been born with a host of congenital anomalies. Although her brain was intact and her limbs appeared strong and healthy, just about everything else was a mess. There were problems with her liver, her intestines, her heart, and her kidneys. She needed tubes to feed her, tubes to remove wastes, and tubes to help her breathe. The trick for Audrey was to keep her alive until she was big enough to tolerate the surgery she needed to repair her multitude of problems. She was already seven months old and had spent her entire life in a hospital. Her mother was young, not even eighteen, single, and incapable of giving Audrey the level of care she needed. What social services wanted was to get her out of the hospital and into a family. The hope was that the added social and emotional stimulation would improve her weight gain and encourage her development. The big question was whether any family could care for her, and we wouldn't know until we saw her.

The medical center was only an hour away, so Bruce and I cleared our schedule for a full Sunday and went to meet Audrey. The hospital had done its best to make the ward a cheerful place. Colorful murals covered the walls, and each room boasted a good selection of toys, videos, and comfortable rocking chairs. But there was no disguising the reality that this was a ward for very sick children. Kids with tonsillectomies and broken legs went elsewhere. On a ward full of children with cancer and heart disease and AIDS, Audrey was far and away the sickest child.

She wasn't really all that small, but in the vastness of the hospital crib, she certainly looked tiny. The tubes running in and out of her body conveyed an image of frailty that we expected but still weren't adequately prepared for. Audrey shared a room with two other children, a little girl of about four with some sort of palsy that twisted her body into a permanent, uncomfortable-looking position and the other, a boy, who'd had a tumor removed from his kidney several months earlier and was now back with a suspicious shadow on a brain scan.

I could overhear the parents of these children talking to family members on the room phone, their panic clear in every word. Before I could concentrate on Audrey, I said a silent prayer of thanksgiving for my noisy, naughty energetic troop at home and wished I had not scolded Ben that morning for tracking mud across the kitchen floor.

Bruce was less intimidated than I by Audrey's tangle of wires and tubes. He worked in a hospital, and although his background was engineering rather than medicine, he knew what all the blips and beeps meant. I was trying to get a mental picture of what having Audrey in our family would entail, and frankly, I was scared to death. When a child comes to me, she usually has been through the worst you can imagine. Now that I had some experience under my belt, I knew I was unlikely to say or do anything to her so awful that I couldn't undo it, but with Audrey it was very different. If I made a mistake, Audrey could die. She would probably die anyway. Even in the short time we spent with her, that fact was all too clear.

Audrey's nurse was very kind and calmly competent. She showed us how the feeding tube worked and some of the finer points of the catheter. Bruce was able to ask intelligent questions and even appeared to understand the answers, but I became more lost by the moment. Only when Audrey was disconnected from some of the machinery and I was able to hold her did I feel somewhat back in control. She wasn't a pretty baby, just sweet and rather placid. I relaxed a bit as I rocked her, but something was wrong. I waited to feel some connection to her, as I had to Shamika, but it just didn't happen. I felt as though I was holding crystal.

We stayed a bit longer, taking careful notes and making out a long to-do list. At last we started for home. Bruce chatted away about the logistics of caring for Audrey, and I felt myself getting angrier by the moment. I couldn't believe he didn't understand how incapable of this I was. Of course, the sensible thing would have been to say so. Bruce might have been surprised and perhaps mildly disappointed, but he certainly wouldn't have disagreed. However, I could not admit that this was more than I wanted to do. Until then, I had not been aware of how much of my identity was tied up in taking really hard kids: kids like Danny and Sara whom no one else much wanted. If I turned my back on Audrey, I knew I would feel like a failure. The question was, Was I willing to risk a baby for ego?

I spent the next few days on the phone, looking into home nursing services and checking with our local fire department about emergency generators. I talked to Susan and the DSS nurse and Audrey's hospital social worker. To no one did I voice my concern or lack of enthusiasm about Audrey. I could barely admit it to myself. Toward the end of the week, I steeled myself for another hospital visit, hoping that Bruce was right, that this whole thing was about organization. I would just follow my to-do list and everything would be fine.

Audrey's room was quiet when I got there. There was usually a bustle of activity, so I was glad for a few minutes alone with her. I looked over her chart with only a vague idea of what the numbers meant. I pulled a chair up to the side of the crib. Audrey was sleeping on the blanket I had brought for her on my last visit. There was a new picture on the wall behind her. It was a page from a coloring book signed "Cousin Emmy." I realized that I knew nearly nothing about her family.

Audrey was restless, not awake but tossing and turning and whimpering. I reached up to smooth her hair back from her forehead and was surprised by how warm she felt. Really warm. Scary warm. I rang the call bell once, and Audrey's nurse scooted into the room.

"Hi! I didn't expect you today," she said. "Are you ready for your first try at inserting the feeding tube?"

"Could you feel her head? She feels awfully warm to me. She's breathing funny too."

The nurse felt Audrey's head and frowned slightly. "Hmmm. She does feel warm. I'm going to check her vitals. I wonder if she's got an infection cooking."

In seconds, the room exploded. There were doctors and nurses everywhere. It was hard to follow the conversations, all of which took place in the medical shorthand that hospital people use, but I got the gist. There was an infection someplace. It was probably pneumonia because Audrey's lungs were congested while her temperature continued to climb.

I felt totally superfluous and unexpectedly panicked. All of a sudden I cared about Audrey, but not in the disconnected way I would feel about any child who was quite ill. I cared about *this* child, Audrey; I didn't want her to die.

A team of residents looked over her chart, drew some blood, had a hurried conference, and with no fanfare wheeled her down the hall to the pediatric intensive care unit. I couldn't visit her there, and since the staff wouldn't have time to talk to me, I slipped quietly out a stairwell exit and headed home. For once I was grateful for the long commute to my house; it gave me time to collect my thoughts.

I spent some time with Karen when I got home, dressing her baby dolls and reading to her. When she fell asleep, I couldn't put off any longer what I knew I had to do. I called Susan and the hospital social worker, and Patty, the DSS nurse, and told them all essentially the same thing: I couldn't take Audrey. Even with a lot of nursing support, even if I had no other kids, this particular child was beyond what I could do. I had often told my older daughters that their mother had surrendered them for adoption because she loved them and knew she couldn't take care of them. For the first time, I understood the magnitude of those words. I understood the fear and the grief and the blow to a mother's sense of self that come from making the decision that I can't. I wish I could, but I can't.

I saved my final call for Bruce. I wasn't angry with him anymore. There was no way for him to know how Audrey scared me when my pride prevented me from admitting it out loud.

Bruce was his usual philosophical self. He hoped she would do well, but he could see how she might be too much for us. There would be another baby we could help. There always was.

I hung up feeling drained but vastly relieved. No one thought I was awful or lazy or stupid. Everyone understood. Being a foster mother didn't mean I needed to be every lost baby's savior.

My list hung lopsided on the refrigerator door. It was smudged a bit and had acquired a patina of peanut butter and ketchup. I only thought a minute before I added Audrey's name and birthday to it. She had never lived here. I had held her only once, but it was enough to make her belong there. I have had several occasions over the years to think about why I couldn't take Audrey and why I found it so hard to say no. This is what I've arrived at: I want to live a life that matters, a life that makes a difference. To do that as a foster parent I have to make sure that every child I say yes to will be better off for the experience of living with me. I am not naïve enough to believe that I can fix every problem or give every child all of what he or she needs. Dan and Sara can both attest to that, but I do believe that each of them left with more than they came with. When I wrote their names on my list I have to believe that, in many ways that matter, all of our lives were enriched.

Chapter

Thirteen

Like a skittish kitten, Sara hovered around the fringes of our family, wanting desperately to be part of us but isolated, both by fear and a lack of experience with anything like us. Having Lucy move on to what we all referred to as her "forever family" only made things worse. Sara was both angry and jealous, a combination that, for her, was deadly. Sara had little experience with anger that didn't lead to violence with the most vulnerable person in the house as the target. The violence always had a sexual element to it.

Sandra, Sara's therapist, was increasingly concerned by some behaviors we had begun to see emerging. More and more often, Sara was pulling out her hair when she was angry or gouging ugly welts in her arms. She was smearing feces, even in school, and much to my dismay, I one day found her in the bathroom, unrolling used sanitary napkins. Supervising the children so they couldn't become involved in her sexualized play was a full-time job. Sandra was not surprised by it, and she did her best to educate me about what to expect and how to respond. I guess I was a slow study: we installed a rather elaborate intercom system to connect the bedrooms and the common areas of the house, the better to keep track of what was going on, but still we didn't admit that there was something seriously wrong. I hung on to the naïve belief that deep down Sara was just fine. I needed to believe that because, in spite of myself, I had fallen hard for this little girl. I talked to Sandra each week about what was going on with Sara and then promptly disregarded all her words of caution and went right on believing that if I treated Sara like a normal child she would *be* normal.

The rest of the family was less enamored than I was and far less tolerant of Sara's more aberrant behavior. The males in particular didn't appreciate Sara's seduction routines and began to avoid her whenever possible.

Spring soccer and baseball started right after Lucy left. All the kids played on one team or another, and it seemed like we spent all our time in the car. It had never been more than an inconvenience before, but Sara, I discovered, was car phobic. Who knows why. Maybe something bad had once happened to her in a car. Whatever the reason, I had only to mention a car trip to anywhere but the grocery or therapy to have Sara turn stiff, completely resistant. I could pick her up and carry her to the car without too much trouble; she was pretty tiny. But once I got her to the car I was out of luck. I had to put her down to open the door, and she would hightail it back to the house with me in hot pursuit. When I snagged her again and toted her back outside, I couldn't get her legs or her waist folded so she would fit in the seat. After several minutes of struggle, I might get the seat belt fastened around her, close the doors, and head back to the driver's door. Without fail, she'd be out of the belt and out the door again before I could get inside. Throughout the entire time she would scream "No, no, no, you can't make me go."

It was exhausting work. It was tempting to think she was just being oppositional, but I never really believed that. Sara was never that oppositional about anything else unless, as with the bathtub, she had good reason to be really scared.

I'm afraid I let the car problem get to me. If Sara was the immovable object, then I was the irresistible force. Almost daily, we would lock horns over getting her in the car. Some days, I won and managed to get out of the driveway before she wrestled out of her seat belt. Other days, she won, and I left her home with Bruce.

It was clear that Sara had something to gain from her outbursts. Everyone's attention was riveted on her. Our trips were controlled by her rage. I tried not to obsess about the car problem, but with my busy schedule it was a considerable inconvenience and getting worse by the day. When it was just my own kids I could usually cope, but I was part of a carpool, and the addition of the two extra children made the situation intolerable. It was mortifying for Angie and Neddy to have their friends privy to some of Sara's more colorful explicatives. I also worried that Sara would develop a schoolyard reputation of being a bit south of normal in terms of mental health.

This situation finally came to a head one day, forcing me to reevaluate how I was handling the whole mess. I was running late (my usual time frame) and feeling a bit out of sorts. As soon as Sara saw the girls packing water bottles and snacks to take in the car, she started to whine. I made no attempt to talk to her or cajole her into cooperating. Instead, I scooped her up under one arm and toted her, like a squawking football, out to the van. With each step, the volume of her howling intensified until it reached an ear-popping level.

With the fervor of one possessed, I dumped Sara into the closest seat belt and snapped it shut, angry but in control. I am fairly certain it was unintentional, but her small sneakered foot snapped up and caught me squarely in the jaw. It really hurt, and that was the final straw. Weeks of car hell were caught in that kick, and I snapped. I unhooked the seat belt and dragged Sara out. This, I thought, must be what crazy feels like. I didn't care what I looked like or who saw me. I was so furious that I only wanted to get Sara inside where I could dish out some appropriate discipline. But Sara, feeling assaulted by her abrupt and harsh removal from the van, beat me to the punch. Before I could put her down, she was raking her face with her fingers and pulling at her hair. Her transformation from angry to hysterical pulled me back to sanity, but it was too late for Sara. Her nails were bitten down to well below her fingertips, but she still managed to leave ugly red furrows. What upset me the most was seeing the long tangle of hair she held in her hand.

"Sara! Stop! We do not hurt ourselves!" I exclaimed. But Sara was beyond hearing. She kept screaming, lost in some frightening faraway place I couldn't reach.

Carrying her inside the house, I dropped to the floor and pulled her into my lap. With my legs wrapped around her legs and my arms crossed firmly across her chest, Sara couldn't move. But she could still scream, and she did, over and over.

Technically, foster parents aren't supposed to restrain kids. It is far too easy to cross the line and really hurt somebody. More than one child has died during restraint by people who were professionally trained. However, we are not told what we *should* do when a kid is out of control. We could call an ambulance and get the child to a hospital, but doing so is just not realistic. Kids who end up in foster care have had a lot of trauma, and tantrums are an everyday occurrence. If foster parents took every raging kid to the E.R., the health care system would grind to a halt. Emergency rooms are not equipped to handle pediatric mental health emergencies, and already there are not enough beds in psychiatric hospitals to handle the kids who are in real crisis. They certainly don't have the resources to deal with anything less serious.

We do the best we can with the resources we have, but every time we hold a kid down to prevent him from hurting himself or somebody else, we risk an abuse charge or worse. You can understand why some families refuse to take the chance and won't keep a kid who tantrums.

As I struggled to get Sara calmed down, into the fray walked Nathan with a friend from college. Matt was a quiet young man, the only child of an artist and a college professor. What must he have thought when he walked into my kitchen? There I sat, my face red and my hair in a wild tangle. Sara's eyes were glazed with terror and rage. I'm sure we looked like an illustration from the *Snake Pit,* the crazed inmate and the equally crazed keeper.

I tried to speak in a normal voice. "Hi, guys," I said. "Excuse me for not getting up. Sara's having a hard time right now, but she'll be better soon. What are your plans today?" My tone was bright and cheerful, as though having a small girl wrapped in a basket hold in the middle of the kitchen floor while a carload of soccer players waited outside was an everyday occurrence.

Nate must have been embarrassed but he never missed a beat. "We were planning on running over to the club to play some golf. Do you need something?"

"If I paid for the golf and sodas, would you run your sisters and the Mitchell girls to soccer practice for me?"

"Sure. We'll be driving right by."

After Nathan and Matt left, Sara and I sat entwined for several minutes, our breathing gradually slowing down as my grip on her loosened.

"I didn't mean to kick you," she said almost inaudibly.

"I know you didn't," I replied.

I felt I needed to say something, but words wouldn't come. The phone rang, but I didn't have the energy to pick it up. Sara and I just sat, my holding turning into an embrace.

Finally, I decided to just come out with it. "Could you talk to me about your problem with the car? If I just knew why you were so scared, maybe I could help."

"I just hate it. I don't have to have a reason, do I?"

"I suppose you don't."

Sara turned to face me, her eyes just inches from mine. "You gonna send me away?"

Her eyes were an indistinguishable color, murky, like the eyes of a newborn.

"I don't send kids away, Sara. Not unless I can't help them."

"You gonna spank me?"

"I don't spank kids either. You know that."

"Do you know where my mom is?" That wasn't the question I expected.

"I don't, sweetie. Remember what I told you? I heard she was in Florida but I'm not really sure. Do you want to see her?"

"I guess. Sometimes I miss her but I don't cry. I just think about her for a while."

"Do you ever wonder if I might take you somewhere and leave you? Like you got taken here?"

Sara gave a nearly imperceptible shrug. I realized something that made me sad. As much as I thought I was empathetic, that I knew what it felt like to be Sara or Dan or Lucy, I really couldn't. My parents were married for over fifty years. My older brother and sister helped raise my younger brother and me. The four of us remain best friends, having dinner together often and talking on the phone almost daily. Before I became a foster parent I took the wealth of having a family for granted. I had never been hungry without the promise of food. I had always been warm enough, held enough, safe enough. I had never been left behind without the promise of a return. Now, I couldn't fully accept the truth of who my children were or where they came from. There were limits to what I could know and absorb, limits that went beyond my finite abilities. I could guess a bit, but I would never know nor did I really want to. I could hold Sara. I could even love her. But I could never know or change her past.

Sara calmed down some, and I sent her outside to play with Karen and some neighborhood kids. I took a glass of iced tea and sat on the deck to watch them. Sara's face was still red and swollen, and she stayed a bit apart from the other girls. Now and then she would laugh a little at something another kid said, but the laughter had a strained quality about it that sounded far from happy. I wondered if part of her problems stemmed from the uncertainty she must have felt about her future. Sharon had completely disappeared from her daughter's life. Annie and Thomas were both in residential programs halfway across the state. For all Sara knew, her father was out of her life.

Earlier in the week I had received a call from Nelson Meyers, a social services attorney who represented DSS when they went to court to request that a judge terminate a person's parental rights to his child. This had to happen before a child was legally freed for adoption. Mr. Meyers had set up an appointment with me to discuss having me testify in the court case that would terminate the parental rights of both of Sara's parents.

Other than a brief stint as a juror a few years earlier, I had never been in court, and, I'll confess, the idea was not appealing. As I've said, I'm an easy crier. Not only would I be expected to sit in a witness box and recount what Sara had told me about the abuse she had endured in her birth home, I would need to do it while looking like a professional, a feat I was not at all certain I could pull off.

Sara's father, I was told, would be there too. I had never met the man, but I had heard enough about him to be afraid of him. I didn't want him to know my name or where I lived, but that was information he would be entitled to if I testified against him.

The girls played on, oblivious to my worries. Karen had just learned to do a somersault. She repeated the maneuver over and over, calling to me, "Look, Mommy! Watch me!" while she tumbled in the grass. Karen had left the toddler stage and was looking like a preschooler. She was a beautiful little girl, with an air of confidence and security that was lacking in my other foster children.

We had heard nothing from Bonnie for months. Her whereabouts remained a mystery. This complicated the process of terminating her parental rights because the legal department of the social services office had to provide evidence to a judge that they had exhausted all means of locating her and notifying her of their intent to terminate her parental rights and release Karen for adoption. Fortunately, Meg was a diligent and thorough caseworker. She called often to let me know what was happening, and she visited with Karen every month. I soon began to look forward to her visits as much for the fact that I liked her as for her role in Karen's life.

Karen's attorney, Sam, kept in touch as well, but until her case went to court in December he really had nothing to do, so he was generally content to call every few months to make sure everything was going well with his client.

And it was going well, I thought as I watched Karen play. She still had some problems separating from me, but I saw this as the result of her age, the coming and going of other children in our home, and her history. Never did I attribute it to a more serious anxiety. She was nearly three, a sweet, charming, and precocious little girl.

When the telephone rang I was tempted to let it go as I had earlier. I was feeling drained from my encounter with Sara and really needed to regroup for a while longer before I could face another request. Because I had Nathan on the road with a car full of kids I couldn't ignore it, but my hello sounded terser than I intended.

"Hi, Kathy," said Sam's familiar voice. "How's Karen doing?"

"Fine," I replied. "She's getting so grown up. You'll have to drop by and see her. I've been thinking about calling you to ask about her court case. December seems so far away. I'm anxious to get it over with. I won't have to testify, will I?"

"That's what I called about, Kathy. It looks like we have a bit of a glitch that may delay things. Bonnie is back, and her attorney claims she's been clean and sober for almost ten months. They're filing a motion to delay this trial and reinstate weekly visits. She's changed her mind about the adoption. It seems she met a man in AA. They're in a long-term relationship, and they want Karen."

For the first time in my life I thought that I really might faint. The blood pounded so loudly in my ears that I missed Sam's next sentence.

"They couldn't really get her, could they?" I asked frantically. "After all that's happened, no judge would take her away from us. Karen doesn't even remember Bonnie."

Sam's voice came back annoyingly calm and rational. I didn't want calm. I didn't want rational. I wanted the world to be as outraged as I was. I wanted Sam to assure me that no judge would take a little girl away from the only family she knew to place her with strangers who had long histories of substance abuse and mental health issues. But Sam was a lawyer. He dealt with facts, not with wishes, and he was honest when he answered me.

"You've done a great job with Karen. No one questions Bruce's or your commitment, but that's not what the judge is going to be looking at. Some of the better judges look primarily at the best interests of the child. In that case, one would probably rule in your favor. Some of the older judges still look at current fitness to parent. In that case, Karen will probably go home."

"Do you know who's hearing the case?"

"Montgomery. It could be better, but it could be worse. She's fair, but I think she tends to side with birth parents when there is a question about custody. But with very young kids, I know she takes into consideration who the psychological parent is. You have to remember, Kathy, this isn't a contest between you and Bonnie. It's going to come down to whether Bonnie is sufficiently rehabbed."

When Bruce got home, he didn't ask what was wrong. Meg had called him at work and told him. He just handed me a bouquet of flowers and pulled me into his arms.

"What do we do?" I whispered.

"What *can* we do?"

"We can move. Would they extradite us from Canada?"

"We've got five other kids and a mortgage. We can't run, Kathy. We have to stay and fight this. We have to believe that if this is meant to be, it will be. If not, then we have to believe we're strong enough to cope."

"Whose bright idea was this anyway?" I ranted in response. "What ever made me think fostering was a good idea? It's a stupid system that only stupid people would have anything to do with. The minute this is resolved with Karen, I'm done. I quit. I'm going back to work. To hell with DSS and to hell with foster care."

"What about Sara?"

"What about her? It's not like anybody is going out of his way to do what's right for her either. She's going to bang around in care until she's so screwed up she ends up in a hospital somewhere, and her creepy father is going to walk because the court system is more worried about his rights than they are about what he did to Sara. I hate this. I wish I had never got involved with any of it. I must have been crazy."

Bruce let me rave on until I had calmed down enough to be rational. Then we just held each other and cried.

Meg called the next morning. She was far more optimistic than Sam about how a custody battle would play out. And it was clear she planned not to go down without a fight. By the end of the week she had enrolled Karen in a bonding study with a therapist who specialized in children with attachment issues. The therapist would observe Karen several times over a month-long period. She would see her in her preschool, at home with Bruce and me, and on visits with Bonnie. At the end of that time she would present her findings and make a recommendation to the court. A judge would place a lot of stock in what this therapist had to say. I was pleased about the study, although it meant that Bonnie would be seeing more of Karen than I was comfortable with. Meg scheduled Bonnie's first visit three days hence, and I was a wreck about it.

I debated about how to dress Karen. On the one hand, I wanted to show off a bit and put her in something fabulous and frilly. On the other, I didn't want to attach any particular importance to the meeting. In the end, I compromised and put Karen in her best overalls and matching shirt. Her hair was quite long and curly. I pulled it up into two corkscrew ponytails. She looked adorable. She looked like Bonnie. Shoot. There wasn't anything I could do about it, but I didn't have to like it.

Bonnie and Meg were waiting in the park when we arrived. It was more than an awkward moment. What, after all, was there for me to say to Bonnie? And how, exactly, was I supposed to present her to Karen? "Here, honey. This is your mommy." Meg rescued all of us by asking Karen if she remembered visiting Bonnie before. Karen pouted but nodded her head and grabbed my hand.

"Don't go, Mama. Stay with me," she pleaded.

It about killed me, but I let go of her hand and kissed the top of her head. "I have to pick up a few things. You're going to stay here and play in the park with Bonnie and Meg. I'll be back soon. Bye-bye."

I walked away and didn't look back.

The next hour was torture. I wandered the streets around the park looking into shop windows. There was a toy store that I seldom shopped at because of the high prices, but that day I did go in. I put in my basket one trinket after another, pretty, glittery little things that I knew Karen would love. Fifteen minutes and fifty dollars later I emerged, feeling foolish and not quite certain just what it was that I was trying to prove. Did I want Bonnie to see how much more I could provide for Karen? Did I want to be sure Meg saw Bruce and me as the more competent parents? Did I hope to ensure Karen's love with some costume jewelry and a plastic princess crown?

As I walked through the park, I caught sight of Bonnie, Meg, and Karen. Karen was holding something up for Bonnie to examine. Bonnie and Meg were laughing. I had a moment of pure jealousy. I didn't want Meg to like Bonnie. I didn't want Bonnie to smooth back my daughter's hair. I didn't want Karen sharing playground treasures with this pretty stranger with the smile that was so familiar it nearly broke my heart. I wanted things the way they were before Bonnie turned up.

Somehow, I swallowed my rage and approached the trio with something that resembled a smile. Bonnie's face revealed nothing, but Karen's lit up when she saw me.

"Look, Momma! Bonnie bringed me a doll, and she did my hair pretty." Karen's hair was indeed recombed. She was clutching a sweet, floppy doll.

I'm ashamed of what happened next. Any time someone wants to tell me what a saint I am, I can pull out this particular memory and poke at it like a wiggly tooth. I knew better. I know what I should have said was something like "How pretty" about the hair and "What a beautiful doll," but I didn't. Like some evil hag from a fairy tale, I pulled out the just-purchased princess crown (which Karen had long coveted) and laid it in her lap with an oh-so-sweet smile. Karen gasped and dropped the doll.

"My crown! You got me my crown!"

Karen was not yet three. She could be forgiven for grabbing the glitz. But what was my excuse?

One look at Bonnie's face drained the anger right out of me. She looked as though someone had let the air out of her. Still, she was big enough to ooh and aah over the toy with far more grace than I had demonstrated.

Meg gave me a very clear "Have you lost your mind?" look and thumbed through her appointment book. I knew she would deal with me later.

"Don't worry about getting a sitter next week," she told me. "I know how busy you are. I'll transport to the next visit."

Of course, my schedule had nothing to do with Meg's offer to drive. With the purchase of one plastic crown I had managed to convince the person I most wanted to impress with my parenting skills that I couldn't be trusted to do the right thing, not just for Bonnie but for Karen too.

In a perfect world, when one feels as dreadful as I did after Karen's visit, life would accommodate and the rest of my day would have been smooth, but this was not a fantasy life. It was real life as a foster parent, and disasters usually occurred in multiples.

While we'd been at the park, I had left Sara, Yolanda, and two new foster kids with a teenager from the neighborhood. Judging from the chaos that greeted me when I got home, she had spent the majority of the afternoon on the phone while the children had fended for themselves.

The two new children were Marisol, a sweet six-year-old of Haitian descent, and Brenda, age four, a pale, overweight, sad little girl who rarely smiled and seldom spoke. Marisol had fared well at home with a young, single mother until a new boyfriend entered the picture. He had taken a belt to Marisol on a couple of occasions, hard enough to leave bruises that were still in the ugly green and purple phase. Marisol could have gone home if her mom had made the boyfriend leave, but she was reluctant to do so. Maybe she was enjoying the life of a teenager without the encumbrance of a child. Maybe she was afraid of him. Whatever the reason, the man who was the abuser stayed, and the kid who was the victim had to leave.

As for Brenda, nothing pleased her much except food. Her depression weighed on everyone in the house. The other kids quickly tired of trying without success to engage her and now, generally, forgot to include her in their games. Her mother was seriously mentally ill and, like Dan's mother, none too bright. I was beginning to suspect that Brenda was slightly retarded as well. Unlike Dan, however, Brenda never got into trouble, probably because it would have taken energy she just didn't have. Brenda was in foster care while her mother was in the hospital trying to stabilize on medication. This wasn't supposed to be a very long placement. I had taken Brenda on hot line, and her social worker was still looking for someone who could keep her long-term. It had already been longer than I wanted, because I simply had too many children. In my opinion, Brenda needed a good assessment, probably long-term intervention services, and a home close to her family so there could be some continuity in care and schooling.

I begrudgingly paid the sitter and got the children settled with crayons and paper. Then I began to attack a mountain of unfolded laundry. Karen scribbled with happy abandon, and Yolanda drew an intricate picture of her school while Brenda made a couple of dark streaks on a piece of paper then slumped in her chair and looked longingly at the cookie jar. This behavior was normal for all of them. But something about Marisol and Sara felt very off.

Sara was acting just too sweet. She hung on my leg, making a pest of herself trying to fold laundry, all the while keeping up a nervous chatter: I was the best mother in the whole world, the best cook, the prettiest. And wasn't it just too bad that it wasn't my day for the car pool because Sara couldn't wait to show me what a good girl she could be in the car.

Sara could be a lot of things but sweet was rarely one of them, and Marisol, on the other hand, was uncommonly quiet. She was a bright child and, like a lot of only children of single parents, used to being spoken to on a very adult level. I often found myself forgetting that Marisol was only six while I debated with her the relative merits of take-out pizza over homemade and how much television was too much for Brenda.

"Okay, you two, what's up?" I said. "Is everything all right, Marisol?"

Two bright spots of color appeared high on Sara's cheeks. She glanced at Marisol with a menacing look that I didn't like one bit. Marisol ducked her head but didn't say anything. It was Sara who spoke.

"Nothing's up," she replied. "Do you want me to help Brenda put her clothes away?"

"I want you to tell me why you look like the cat that swallowed the canary."

Both girls looked puzzled.

"Sara, I want you to sit right at this table and color for a few minutes. Karen, Yolanda, and Brenda, you all sit here too. Marisol, I want to see you in the den."

Our den is a dark, cozy room isolated from the rest of the house. It's a good place for talking about things that are hard to discuss in the glare of bright lights and prying eyes.

"Did you know," I began with a sick feeling in my stomach, "that there are two kinds of secrets, Marisol? There's a good kind, like when it's somebody's birthday and you know what she's getting. That's a fun secret, and thinking about it makes you feel good. Then there's the bad kind of secret. When Leon told you not to tell your grandmother how you got the bruises on your leg, well, that was a bad secret. You needed to tell someone what had happened. Right now, you look like a little girl who just might have a secret. Am I right?" Marisol nodded, ever so slightly. "Do you want to tell me about it?"

Marisol fingered a small cross that she was wearing. It was Sara's cross. The churning in my stomach picked up speed. I waited in the quiet. I could hear the clock ticking and the soft murmur of girls' voices in the kitchen. I didn't hurry Marisol. For a change, I felt like I had all the time in the world.

"Sara wants me to touch her. You know, in her private parts. I didn't want to. Honest. She said if I told you she was gonna tell that it was me who broke your teapot."

"When did this happen, sweetie?"

"It happens a lot. Whenever we play upstairs she takes her pants off and wants me to put toys and stuff in her."

"Have you been doing that?"

Marisol nodded miserably.

"Is that why she gave you the cross, so you wouldn't tell?"

Marisol gave another nearly imperceptible nod.

We sat together for another ten minutes, during which I talked about our bodies belonging to just us and how sometimes people didn't understand that and would try to talk us into doing things that we didn't want to do. I talked about how to say no and about mixed-up good and bad feelings. I'm not sure how much of what I was saying really meant anything to Marisol. She was just a skinny little kid; if someone wanted to touch her, he probably would.

A lifetime ago I was just a regular mom who had regular conversations with her kids about regular things. Even the occasional irregularity was rattled off with a smugness that came from the certainty that it was all for show. The vulgar, seamy side of life could never touch my family. We lived behind the securely locked door of normal and plenty. Now everything was tilted a bit. When we said yes the first time to the foster care system, we unlocked the door and let the snake in.

I sent Marisol out to join the others and heated up some acidic coffee in the microwave. Sara kept shooting glances my way, anxiety printing an H between her eyes. I had to talk to her but not then. Not when anger was being replaced by fear as the reality of the situation seeped into my waterlogged brain.

Marisol had been molested, in my house, on my watch. No matter how you looked at it, ultimately I was responsible. I knew what Sara's behaviors were. Homes had been shut down for less. I had to call Marisol's worker and Sara's. I had to call Sara's therapist, Sandra. I had to hope to God that Bonnie's lawyer didn't catch even a whiff of what was going on. I nearly lost Karen over Danny. Now she could be at risk because of Sara.

What really bothered me was not just the thought of what could happen to me and my family but the knowledge that there was some underlying truth to any concerns that could be raised. Being a foster parent meant I could never be certain when one of the kids I offered a haven to would make the jump from victim to perpetrator. My older kids, the ones still living at home, were smart and savvy and able to take care of themselves, at least physically, but I couldn't guarantee the safety of any of my little ones, not without turning my house into a fortress and myself into the keeper of the keys.

Right in the middle of my deliberations Angie, Neddy, and Ben piled in from soccer practice filled with news of tournaments and schedules that I couldn't quite absorb.

"Hey, guys," I said with enthusiasm I didn't really feel. "I have a great idea for supper, but the deal is you have to make it and clean up the mess."

Three sets of eyebrows raised simultaneously.

"How do banana splits sound?"

All three began talking at once.

"Who are you and what have you done with our mother?"

"It's organic spinach ice cream, isn't it?"

"Don't ask any questions. Just get out the bowls. She could sober up any minute."

Though eight kids and a couple of cartons of ice cream didn't produce absolute quiet, I was left alone long enough to make phone calls. I got in contact with Susan, my caseworker, first. She listened carefully, interrupting only to make sure she understood exactly what had happened.

"First of all," she said, "you did the right thing. You took care of the kid, then called us. You've been careful, but Sara is more creative than most kids about getting under the radar. Why don't I talk to both of the girls' workers and you get ahold of the therapist and see what she thinks? Sara's a pretty damaged kid. Maybe she needs more structure than a foster home can provide."

I started to protest but Susan cut me off. "I'm not making a recommendation. I'm just thinking out loud. Talk to the therapist and I'll get back to you in the morning, and we'll see what kind of plan we can come up with that will keep everybody safe. Before we hang up, how are you doing? You're not thinking about bailing out on us, I hope."

That was exactly what I was thinking, but now was not the time to get into it.

"If we decide to bail," I said, "you'll be the first to know. I'll talk to you tomorrow."

I left an urgent message for Sandra, and she responded within the hour. Her recommendation was what I both feared and hoped for. She wanted Sara in a psychiatric hospital as soon as we could locate an empty bed. I had had several other kids in crisis over the years, so I was aware that finding a hospital bed for a six-year-old who is a threat to other children is nothing like finding a hospital bed for a child who needs her appendix out. There are very few hospitals that have the resources to deal with kids like Sara. The ones that do have waiting lists ranging from several days to several weeks. A kid needs to have made a real suicide attempt to classify as an emergency. So I expected to run into the same red tape and delays that I had run into previously.

Fortunately, I was wrong. I never knew what strings Sandra pulled, but she called me at nine the next morning with news of an opening at Northwoods Medical Center for that afternoon. I had sent Sara to school, in part because I didn't know what else to do with her. I was glad she wasn't home because after I spoke to Sandra, I broke down and cried. Eventually, I would cry for Marisol and what she had been through, but for now my tears were all for Sara. I packed a single suitcase with the things Sandra suggested I send. Two pairs of pajamas, a robe, and slippers. Three pairs of pants, three shirts, socks, and underwear. She could have a stuffed bear and some pictures but nothing else. I couldn't send her comb or her toothbrush. Children can hurt themselves with those things. The hospital would provide these items and supervise their use.

Bruce called several times to check on me. He couldn't get away from work, but he said he would stop at the hospital on the way home to check on Sara. I had to tell him not to bother. Visitation was only from seven to eight. If he went at five, he wouldn't be allowed to see her.

I called Sara's school and let them know I was picking her up early and that she wouldn't be in for a while. I knew that, at some point, I would need to let them know where she was going, but I just couldn't say the words yet. They probably guessed, based on Sara's behavior, and were kind enough not to ask. A friend from my foster parent support group offered to come to the house to supervise the other children, and I went to pick up Sara. Before I put her in the car, I held her close for a moment. I took a breath and told her where she was going and why. The tantrum I anticipated never came. Sara stood stoically, her face unreadable. When I let go of her she marched to the side of the van and waited for me to pull open the door. For a change, she climbed quietly into her seat and fastened her seat belt without help. We drove to the hospital in virtual silence. Sara refused to answer my questions and had none of her own. Not until we pulled into the parking lot and I turned off the ignition did she break down and sob like the very little child she was.

Chapter

Fourteen

The children's psychiatric ward at Northwoods Medical Center was located in a shabby old building several blocks from the main campus. It was due to be phased out within the next few years, and little money was being spent on it for anything but necessary maintenance. While the pediatric medical wing was bright and welcoming, with lovely murals and an array of wonderful toys, the psychiatric ward was painted in those nauseating shades of institutional beige and green so common in old buildings. There were charts on the walls reminding children of the hospital's rules and consequences and a few painted pictures with curled edges.

Sara held on to the tail of my jacket while I followed the directions that brought us to the ward where she'd be staying. We rang the call bell and waited to be escorted inside. A dour-faced aid peered at us through a small viewing window in the door. Not until the moment I heard the click-click of the lock's tumblers did the reality hit me. Sara, six-year-old Sara, who liked baby dolls and *Sesame Street*, strawberry ice cream and the Beatles, was on a locked psychiatric ward.

I heard a sound behind me and turned to find Bruce standing there. He must have guessed what this would be like for Sara and me and had slipped away from work to join us. Sara barely looked at him, but I was never so glad to see anyone in my life. Sara's new caseworker, Patricia, was waiting for us in the intake office. She had met Sara only twice since being assigned her case a few months earlier, but she needed to be there to sign the necessary admittance paperwork.

Bruce, Sara, and I followed the aid to a small office. Bruce and I took seats but Sara stood just inside the door of the office, refusing to move. She was wearing a new dress, and her hair was carefully braided. I was glad she looked so cute. The fates, I thought, were generally kinder to well-tended children. A young woman in street clothes came up behind Sara and said firmly, "Your parents have to fill out some paperwork. I'll take you to your room and help you put your things away." Sara went with her without an argument.

The intake worker, Cynthia, had gotten insurance information and Sara's history from Patricia, but she wanted to talk to Bruce and me about the most recent events at our house. I did my best to just give the facts, but as usual I was a dismal failure at keeping anything like a detached exterior when I talked about my kids. When my voice cracked, Cynthia handed me a box of tissues with a sympathetic smile.

"What can you do for her?" I asked.

"To tell you the truth, not much," Cynthia answered. "She may benefit from an antidepressant although I don't like to use them on such a young child. We'll try to get her stable and see if she can function at home."

"How long will she be here?"

"At seven hundred dollars a day, the insurance company will only approve three days at a time," Cynthia said. "They really start to balk after a couple of weeks. We'll try to get her home by then."

We found Sara sitting on her bed with a pile of things on either side of her. The woman who had taken her to her room was going through Sara's suitcase. She introduced herself as Michelle and told us she would be Sara's "shadow" while she was there. She congratulated us on packing so well, putting nothing in Sara's bag she could use to injure herself.

We stayed for only a few minutes, then rose to leave. Our departure wasn't easy. Bruce's eyes were bright and his voice husky when he said good-bye to Sara. He seldom hugged her because she was so obviously uncomfortable with him, but he did so now and she clung to him so tightly that he had to pry her hands from around his neck.

"We have to go now, honey. We'll call you tomorrow, and Kathy will visit in a couple of days." Bruce cupped Sara's face in his hands and kissed her forehead.

I wrapped my arms around Sara's pencil-thin body until I trusted myself not to cry.

"I'm going to miss you, Sara. Who's going to help me find my glasses and my car keys?"

"Kathy, I don't wanna stay. I want to go home. I'll try harder this time. I promise." Sara's voice had that frantic edge that signaled the start of a tantrum.

"It's not about trying, Sara. We have to keep everybody safe. Including you."

"You hate me. You're glad to get rid of me. Now you can be with your own kids, and you don't have to bother with me."

Michelle broke in. "Bruce and Kathy are leaving, Sara. You'll see them soon. She looked pointedly at us, then the door. We took the cue and left with Sara's screams slicing through the air.

The last thing we needed was a visit with Sara every few days added to a schedule that was already too full. The bonding specialist in Karen's case, Lorraine Williams, had arranged to meet Bruce, Karen, and me for the first time, and I was cleaning like a mad woman. The house wasn't dirty, but it did seem to get buried under a mountain of gym bags and books. The laundry was never quite done, nor was the sink ever empty for long.

I wanted Lorraine to see us as the perfect family. We weren't, but we were hoping to cover up the worst of our flaws.

When she arrived the next Tuesday morning, the socks were sorted (for which I had paid the sitter an extra five dollars), the dishes were done, and the gym bags were in the mudroom. Angie and Neddy were keeping the other children occupied. Karen looked adorable in a new dress and matching hair ribbons. If you discounted the fact that I had one kid on a psychiatric ward and one who seldom spoke, we looked like anybody else's too-large family enjoying the pale winter sunshine.

Having Lorraine visit gave me a glimpse of what it must feel like to be a client of social services. Now, it was my family being observed, my parenting. But I could ill afford to show the anxiety

I felt. I needed Lorraine to think I was perfect, and perfect I was going to be.

And I would have been. I'm nearly certain I could have pulled it off if only Angie and Neddy hadn't got into an argument over who was in charge, if Ben hadn't put a snowball through the neighbor's window, if the phone hadn't rung half a dozen times, and if Marisol hadn't put her tooth through her lip. Then Karen wanted juice, and Brenda began to sulk until I finally threw up my hands and let it go. What Lorraine saw was what was real, and she could like it or not.

Things got easier after that. Angie and Neddy took the girls out to play, and Ben took Karen to the grocery store so that Bruce and I could talk to Lorraine about how being an adoptive and foster family had changed us all and how some of those changes were good and healthy and some weren't. We talked about stress and working and how strange it was to be a stay-at-home mom with small children while in my mid-forties. We were still talking when Ben brought Karen home, complete with sticky hands and a chocolate smile.

"Mama! Look! Ben bought me a pinwheel, and he got one for Marisol and one for Brenda and one for Yolanda."

I blew into the pinwheel and it turned madly, the red and yellow fans spinning rapidly until they blended into an orange circle. Just like us, I thought. A bit of this and a bit of that, out of control sometimes but somehow spinning together in a way that worked.

Meg called shortly after Lorraine left to see how things had gone and to talk about the next several visits. She brought up the princess crown, as I knew she would. Although she was easier on me than she probably should have been, Meg made it clear that she had expected better. This wasn't a contest between the have and the have-nots, and I couldn't turn it into one. I promised to do better, sounding eerily to my ears like Sara.

My chance to prove myself came on Thursday. Meg was going to be in court in the morning, so she needed me to drive Karen to her scheduled visit with Bonnie. I might even need to stay with the two of them until Meg could get there. Far be it from me to suggest that Meg might have been a bit duplicitous or that she might have set things up so that Bonnie, Karen, and I would have to spend an hour together without anyone to monitor our conversations, but that is, in fact, what happened.

In the ten months since Bonnie had disappeared from Karen's life, she had had another baby. She brought two-month-old Carley with her on this visit. Carley was a pretty little thing, just starting to smile and coo. I was grateful that Bonnie didn't introduce her as Karen's sister, just as Carley. Karen was enchanted with Carley for about sixty seconds, and then the playground beckoned. I offered to mind Carley while Bonnie pushed Karen on the swings.

The hour melted away, and there was still no sign of Meg. Bonnie and I staked out a spot in the shade and settled Karen with juice and crackers while Bonnie fed Carley. Karen chatted away, showing off her new ability to name colors.

"How did you do that?" Bonnie said, looking genuinely puzzled.

"Do what?" I said.

"Teach her colors and things like that. How do you know what to do? I feel like I'm always guessing. I don't know how I'll ever teach Carley to tie her shoes or write her name."

"Actually, when I brought my first child home I had no idea what to do with him," I replied. "I was scared to death. But my mother and my sister helped a lot, and Bruce's brothers and sisters all had kids. I don't think any of us are supposed to raise kids alone. It's too hard."

Bonnie pulled the nipple from Carley's mouth and put her over her shoulder for a burp.

"Your instincts are good, Bonnie. I'm sure you'll do just fine with Carley."

"But not with Karen?"

"It won't be my call."

Meg was nowhere to be seen, and I needed to go home. We gathered up our things and stood facing each other. "You must hate me," Bonnie said.

"How can I hate you? You're Karen's mother. Do you hate me?"

"How can I hate you? You're her mother too."

I really wanted to squeeze in a visit with Sara. Too much time had already gone by since I had dropped her off, and I'd been feeling like I was one of the many neglectful parents I'd seen through the years, who, having dumped their kids into someone else's hands, proceed to forget all about them. That wasn't the case. I thought about Sara all the time. I just seldom had the necessary four-hour block of time it took to get to Northwoods, visit, and get back.

"Ah," whispered a nagging little voice, "you would be there if it were Karen, wouldn't you? You would be there if it were Angie or Neddy or one of your sons. You would never have left Ben alone." The voice was right. I called every day, but that wasn't the same as a visit, and Sara and I both knew it.

I finally made it in to see Sara on Monday. I went through the same process with the locks and escorts that I had when I had dropped her off. Experience did not make it easier.

There was a handwritten sign on Sara's door: "Female Attendants Only," in bright red letters. That was ominous. Sara was waiting for me in the visitation room. In a place notable for its grimness, this room stood out as remarkably grim. While the other pediatric wards were awash with bright colors, the psychiatric ward was further wounded with old furniture patched with silver duct tape and curtainless windows. The room whispered insults: This is what we think you are worth. This is who you are.

Physical illness is an assault on an innocent victim, but mental illness is different; it is a character flaw. Did the powers that be believe that if they made the place ugly enough, the children would shape up so they could go home? While I can't speak for the children, I know that just walking in the door filled me with such despair I could barely breathe. I longed to open a window or play some Mozart. I wanted to paint the walls a bright blue or hire someone to tap-dance in the hallway. I wanted out.

I found Sara slouched in the corner of a sofa in the visitor's lounge wearing a nasty expression and somebody else's T-shirt.

"Hey, cookie," I said with a heartiness that echoed falsely in the gloomy space.

"How come you didn't come visit me? You said you'd come. You lied." Sara's words were angry, but her face looked more sad than mad.

"It's been five days. I'll bet you've been lonely. Have you met anybody to play with?"

"They're all boys and they're mean. I don't have anybody to play with. The staff is mean too. They always take away my points when I didn't do anything, so I didn't get to go roller skating and everybody else did."

I had to smile. Sara sounded so much like any six-year-old feeling sorry for herself.

Cynthia, the intake worker, poked her head around the corner. "When you're finished, I'd like to have a word with you," she said to me.

I decided not to discuss the subject of points with Sara. She needed a mom more than she needed another teacher or therapist just then. So I talked instead about what was going on at home and at school. As we talked, Sara kept inching closer and closer to me until finally she was perched in my lap. We spent the rest of our time together rocking and talking, neither one of us wanting to bring up anything that might hurt or intrude upon the good feelings.

All too soon, it was time for me to leave. I expected a good-bye tantrum but it never came. Sara shut down when I kissed her, her eyes glazed with tears she refused to shed. The adult control bothered me far more than any childish tears would have.

The next three weeks alternately crawled and galloped by. Lorraine conducted what must have been an exhausting schedule of meetings with both Bonnie and Carley's father, Scott, and with Bruce and me, both with and without Karen. Her questions were probing and often hit on topics I hadn't given a lot of thought to, such as what I planned to tell Karen about her birth family and about the circumstances of her coming into foster care and how we would deal with the existence of siblings she didn't know.

Angie and Neddy were older than Karen when they came to us and well aware of their own rocky histories. They knew they had birth siblings they had never seen, but, at least for now, both girls seemed able to deal with the knowledge. I know they were hurt by the lack of consistent contact with their birth mother. We had offered her a liberal open-adoption agreement with a lot of visitation, but she never took advantage of it. I wanted to avoid the pain of looking forward to visits that never happened for Karen. Contact with her birth family would be consistent and dependable, or there would be none at all.

What happened when Lorraine met with Bonnie and Scott I didn't know. I was more than a bit curious, but Lorraine shared nothing with us, even when I came right out and asked.

Ninety-five percent of fostering is taken up by the mundane tasks of cooking and cleaning and bathing children. The other five percent is made up of the adrenaline rush of children arriving or leaving and lives being changed by the turn of a phrase or the slash of a pen. Over a short week in January it felt like a year's worth of adrenaline had been used up. Sara was being released from the hospital, and her exit interview would be on Friday. Our final meeting with Lorraine was scheduled for Wednesday. Bruce needed to plan time off from work to be present at both meetings, and I needed child care.

Lately, I was relying more and more on Neddy to fill in when I couldn't be home. She was more responsible than any other sitter I could get and much more aware of the kids' special needs. I often felt guilty about relying on my children to help out as much as they did, especially Neddy, but as adults I see five people who all know how to change a diaper and fix a bottle, wash a load of clothes, and prepare a meal. I hope that the trade-off has been worth it to them.

Shortly after Sara had come to us her therapist ordered a complete battery of psychological and educational tests for her. The results came as no surprise to anyone. Sara was quite bright, strong in verbal skills, and possessed nearly no ego strength. She saw the world as dangerous and unpredictable and adults as unavailable and unkind. She possessed a frightening amount of rage and hostility mixed with significant depression. She displayed a number of suicidal thoughts and a tendency to dissociate when she felt threatened or overwhelmed. Sara came out of the testing with a laundry list of diagnoses, one of which was chronic maladjustment to family life. I wondered what brain surgeon came up with that bit of wisdom. Given Sara's family life, "chronic maladjustment" seemed like a prudent course. I guess I dismissed a good deal of what the testing showed because of both my distrust in the whole process and a certain amount of denial. I thought it was presumptuous to diagnose Sara just then and far too early to write her off. Surprisingly, the team that tested her agreed with me and recommended retesting when she had been in a stable placement for a year. I'm not at all sure they would have considered our particular family a stable placement, but since we were all Sara had, we would have to do. The time she was in Northwoods seemed as good as any to do the repeat testing. The results would be given to us, along with a discharge plan, at the Friday interview.

That day Bruce and I arrived early at the hospital and hung around in an elegant meeting room while Sara's care team assembled. I wish I could say they had made some huge breakthrough or discovered the magic bullet that could cure what ailed my poor

Sara, but of course there was nothing of the sort. The meeting was just a sorry repetition of Sara's last testing. She was essentially unchanged: still angry, still depressed, still flirting with thoughts of killing herself. The one positive change was in her view of adults. She admitted to trusting and liking Sandra, Bruce, and me. But that trust didn't extend to her view of the rest of the world. She didn't see other children as anything but thieves of the time and attention she thought should be hers exclusively.

In the team's view, Sara was a threat to herself and to others. They would approve sending her back home with us with medication and continued therapy with Sandra, but no one seemed to hold out much hope for her to get better in that scenario. The team's suggestion was to begin the search for an appropriate residential psychiatric placement.

Bruce needed to get back to work, so there was no opportunity for us to process what we had heard together. As I drove home, the words of the psychologist bounced around inside my quiet car. I loved so many things about Sara, but I had to admit that much of what I loved wasn't who she was but rather who I thought she could be. The question was, What was I willing to risk in order to save a kid who looked so lost? Who was I willing to risk?

By Monday, Bruce and I had arrived at a decision. Actually, Bruce arrived at the decision, and I agreed because I couldn't see another option that didn't involve throwing a six-year-old kid to the wolves. We would pick Sara up and bring her home. We would give medication and therapy one more try and pour on the one-on-one attention. We would keep a hawklike watch over her.

Sara was waiting in her room when I arrived at the hospital. She had fewer clothes than I remembered sending her with and a lot more junk. We now owned a lifetime supply of the kinds of projects that are produced in art therapy: clay pots and beaded necklaces. Sara had no tearful good-byes. She had made no friends on the ward, and I suppose the staff was so used to the comings and goings of children that these endings were too routine to attract much notice. There were a couple of hurried "Oh, you're leaving today? Well, see you" kind of statements but that was all— no fanfare and no fuss. Most of these kids were regulars, and I'm fairly certain everyone knew they hadn't seen the last of Sara.

At home, though, a party awaited us. Neddy had baked a cake and Angie had made a welcome-home banner. We ate pizza and sang a very off-key version of "Happy Welcome to You." The weird thing was that we truly were glad to have Sara back. She was going to complicate things in immeasurable ways and make a house already teeming with chaos a good deal more chaotic, but, like all the kids who came to stay, we would somehow separate how she acted from who she was. Who she was, was one of us. And we loved her dearly.

Chapter

Fifteen

❖

As it turned out, Sara's presence *did* complicate things immeasurably. She didn't want me out of her sight for a moment, and she was taking an antidepressant that caused her to have very vivid and scary nightmares. I was up with her several times at night and beginning to feel the effects of sleep deprivation. By Wednesday morning, the day of Lorraine's visit, I was tired and cranky and as jumpy as a flea. Bruce was as anxious as I, although he did a better job of hiding it. We got into one of those little sniping matches that only couples who have been married for many years can manage to pull off with the proper amount of venom. I hadn't made any plans to farm the kids out to various friends and neighbors, not because I didn't see the necessity but because I just hadn't had the time. I blamed him and he blamed me, and by the time Lorraine arrived, ten minutes late, we were both ready to sell the farm and move to Australia. Alone.

But the familiar routine of making tea and welcoming a guest settled us down. By the time Lorraine pulled an astonishingly lengthy
report from her briefcase, we felt considerably better and were ready
to face whatever was coming. She had only one report for Bruce and
me to share. I'm a very quick reader whereas Bruce is slow and me-
thodical. Waiting for him to finish each page was pure torture.

Bruce and I looked at each other, our arguments of the morning long forgotten. There was an odd moment of letdown. So
much worry and so many sleepless nights, wondering if each day
with Karen would be the last, were over, not with blaring trumpets
or courtroom drama but with a written report and a cup of tea. For
a moment, I couldn't think what to do next, but I was saved by the
bell, literally. Meg called and then my mom and my sister. Bruce's
mom was next and then the minister called. Within an hour, the
word was out. I could say the words "our daughter, your sister, your
niece, your granddaughter" and they were real things. Bonnie was
willing to sign a surrender. There wouldn't be a trial. Still we knew
that our gain was Bonnie's loss, as devastating to her as it was joy-
ous to us. I had feared her, been jealous of her; I had even hated her
on occasion. But now I wished I could call her and let her know
how much her sacrifice meant to Karen and to us. I wanted to let
her know that I knew what this had cost her and that I was grateful. I wanted to tell her that Karen would always know how brave
her mother was and how much she loved her.

It was nearly over, but before we had time to celebrate, our attention was diverted by another crisis with Sara. The hoopla surrounding our upcoming adoption of Karen hadn't been easy for
Sara. It wasn't so much that we weren't paying as much attention to
her as we needed to when she returned home, although that was

probably true. More troubling to her, I think, was that the adoption highlighted her own lack of security about her future. Sara had no family fighting for her and no one to visit her or buy her special gifts that the other children didn't also get. Her social worker was nice enough, but she didn't have much to do except wait for an adoption worker to be assigned. Inside, Sara must have been seething. Her anger showed in her usual mix of behaviors. She smeared feces on the toilet seat at school and was found one day sitting under her desk carving welts into her arm with the end of a broken pen.

I have to wonder how I failed to take note of how serious the situation was. Was I simply too busy preparing for Karen's adoption? Or did I not see because I just didn't want to? And what choice did my blind eye leave Sara with besides a grand gesture, something we couldn't ignore?

I confess that I didn't know when or how it happened until several days after the fact. I might not have learned about it at all if Meg had not stopped by with some adoption papers that needed my signature. Meg had been on duty when Brenda had come into care on a hot-line call and she had brought her to us. While I looked over the papers, Meg chatted with Brenda. Much to my surprise, Brenda chatted back.

"I'll bet you have a good time here at Kathy's house with all the little girls to play with," Meg said. "What do you like to do the best? I hear you like the dollhouse."

"I do, and I like the cookies too," answered Brenda. Meg laughed.

"I'll bet you do. Is there anything you don't like?" Meg was referring to food, but that wasn't how Brenda heard the question.

"I don't like to play with Sara. Her wants to be inside my underpants."

We had the safeguards in place but it was all for show. We weren't a hospital or a treatment facility. We were a busy family with kids running in and out and up and down all day. In spite of our best intentions, we couldn't watch everybody all the time. This time our inattention had cost Brenda her innocence. She seemed more annoyed than scarred, but I wasn't fooled for an instant. These things come back to haunt us.

Fortunately, Meg was there. Arrangements were quickly made to get Sara back in the hospital while we waited for a bed to open up in the only long-term treatment program for children as young as she. It would likely take weeks, if not months, for a bed to become available. So, in the meantime, while the rest of us went out to eat and attended school concerts and ball games, Sara would wait on a locked ward at Northwoods.

The absolute unfairness of it all got to me whenever I contrasted Sara's life with the lives of the other children she should have been in school with. I could forget for a while, but it always came back. I found myself crying at odd moments, when I would realize I had set a place at the dinner table for her.

Losing Sara, for this is what her hospitalization felt like to me, was a last straw. I began to think seriously about returning to work when Karen started preschool in the fall. Foster care was not for the weak, and that was exactly what I was, weak and lacking and sick of the whole thing. My screwup with Sara had cost far more than I was willing to spend. I needed to be able to sleep at night without the voices of children calling to me for salvation that I couldn't offer.

So we decided to take a bit of a foster care break. Marisol's mother had gotten rid of her bad-news boyfriend, and Marisol had gone home. Brenda had an aunt turn up who seemed not only willing but also anxious to raise her, and Brenda was packed and ready to go. Yolanda's mother was back on medication and stable, and Yolanda had gone home too. For the first time in several years, our house was nearly empty, except for our own children.

So why wasn't I happy? After weeks of wanting to do something else, my chance was here. Why wasn't I polishing up my résumé and calling my old boss? Why was I packing up Karen's outgrown dresses instead of giving them away? What the heck was wrong with me? I visited with Sara when I could, although not as often as I probably should have. As winter turned into an icy spring, even my twice-monthly trips became difficult to manage. Still, I kept going, although my title as her foster mother was no longer legitimate. She simply had no one else.

The trial to terminate Sara's parents' legal rights to their child was scheduled for April. No one could locate Sara's mom, but that didn't stop the case from going forward. I received my subpoena to testify right after Easter. I was very nervous about going into court although her social services attorney spent several hours preparing me for the experience.

A storm was forecasted for the day of the trial, and I'll admit to praying for something dramatic enough to close the courthouse, but I wasn't that lucky. We got just enough precipitation to ensure a sloppy commute and trouble finding a parking space because of the snow removal.

Waiting to be summoned into court was like old home week arriving at a family reunion. I knew several of the lawyers and all of the social workers who were waiting for their cases to be called.

Even one of the defendants looked familiar to me: I'd had her children in care a few years prior.

As the hours passed, I calmed down some, but then my name
was called and my stomach started churning. I really began to regret
that last cup of coffee. I was called to the witness box, took my oath,
and was seated. For the first time, I saw the man who had abused
Sara. I'm not sure what I expected. Certainly not this ordinary-
looking guy, dressed in jeans and a frayed shirt and with hands that
looked none too clean. For an instant I felt sorry for him, surrounded
as he was by men in expensive suits and so clearly out of place. Then
I remembered what he had done to Sara, and my pity evaporated. I
sat up a little straighter and refused to let my voice shake. I was prepared for the questions from the state lawyer. I answered them truth-
fully. I repeated the things Sara had told me about life with her
father and talked about what her behaviors were like in my house. I
was cross-examined, but the questions were brief and respectful.
I was dismissed after less than two hours on the stand.

I walked to my car, feeling better than I had in months. I was finally able to put my guilt about being unable to help Sara behind
me. I could admit that I would never be her mother in the way I'd
hoped, but I had told her story to the people who needed to hear
it. I had looked at her father and said the equivalent of "This is
what you did. This is why Sara is where she is. You are responsible.
She will never go back to you, and you will never hurt her again."
To the end, I did what I could for Sara.

I was different after that day. I wasn't so much harder as I was more
pragmatic. It took more to shake me. As the months went by, I

found myself not only refraining from taking the break from foster care that I thought I wanted but rather taking kids that would have scared me before. I took a couple of runaway teens and two kids from the same ward Sara had been on at Northwoods.

One afternoon, a girl who had just been picked up by the police as a runaway was brought to our house. She was scheduled to see the judge in the morning. Most of the time, kids like Naomi get sent to a juvenile detention center rather than a foster home, but juvey is one tough place and Linda's social worker was afraid she'd get hurt there. Naomi was, after all, only eleven. She walked in the door with an attitude in every step, looked around, and snorted. "I ain't staying here, you know. You can't fuckin' make me stay."

"I have no intention of making you stay, honey," I answered. "The way I see it, you've got a choice. You can walk out the door right now. I won't try to stop you. If you're lucky, the police will pick you up, and you'll spend the night in juvey. If you're not so lucky, you'll hitch a ride, and the police will pick up what's left of you with a shovel in a couple of weeks. Or you can stay here tonight. The food is good and the sheets are clean. It's up to you."

Naomi blustered, but she took my offer. She didn't turn into Pollyanna, but she was civil for the evening and she didn't try to run. She even thanked me when she left, although she did steal two of Angie's new CDs. I guess you win some and you lose some.

I was thinking about all of this one night, after Sara had left, as I put the finishing touches on dinner. I also was wondering about two little girls, sisters, I had just read about in the paper. They were in the car when their parents were arrested on interstate drug charges. The article had stated that the children were in the custody of DSS and would be placed in foster care. I wondered who would get them and if they would have to be separated. I remembered how hard that had been on Angie and Neddy.

The ringing phone woke me from my reverie. I answered it a little absentmindedly, my thoughts still wandering while I stirred spaghetti sauce.

It was a fairly brief conversation, and I hung up feeling more animated than I had in the past several weeks.

"Hey, Angie," I yelled up the stairs. "Would you come finish the spaghetti for me? I need to pull out some clothes from the attic. Neddy, could you make up the extra beds in the little girls' room? Ben, I could use a hand in the kitchen. We'll need to set another place at the table. In fact, we need two extra places. We've got two little girls coming." I climbed the stairs to the attic, humming a Raffi tune and smiling broadly.

Our house was again bustling with the activity of a gaggle of girls. Bruce and I had been granted the status of an exception home, which gave us permission to have more than the six children under the age of eighteen usually allowed by DSS. Although my youngest son, Ben, was still in high school, he was over that magic age limit of eighteen and no longer counted on our census. That meant I could take three foster children in addition to my three adopted daughters and an additional two children in an emergency. DSS has a lot of emergencies.

By early summer we had an odd little crew playing in the sand-box. Samantha was an adorable two-year-old who looked like a pixie. She was generally a joy to have around, but a couple of times a week something would set her off and she would have a tantrum. Not a regular two-year-old tantrum but a spectacular, screaming, biting, tear-the-curtains-off-the-wall tantrum that lasted for hours. She might calm down a bit, but it was only to catch her breath before the next assault. I wasted no time in calling Sara's therapist to see if she would see Samantha for me. Sandra doesn't gener-ally see two-year-olds, but she recommended a colleague of hers, Jim Simpkin, who specialized in attachment disorders in tod-dlers. Jim had been Tyler's therapist years earlier. He had done as good a job as possible with Ty, and I was pleased to work with him again.

Sandra was, however, seeing another of my little girls, six-year-old Sylvia. Sylvia came into care with a paper bag full of psychiatric medications, no hair, and a diagnosis of anorexia. There was some suspicion she was of limited intelligence, but after a day with Sylvia, I knew that was simply not true. She had some speech prob-lems that made her difficult to understand, but she was certainly bright. She had to be bright to figure out ways to thwart my con-stant efforts to get her to eat. A lot of kids who have been neglected have food issues, but usually they eat everything in sight, worried that it may not be available later. I had never had a child who re-fused to eat anything but applesauce and blueberries or one who wouldn't drink anything but the juice from a melted Popsicle.

Fortunately, I really liked both girls. They were loving children and not a threat to anyone but themselves. Otherwise, I never could have done it; they were so much work—even though torn curtains and eating disorders seemed like a vacation after Sara.

Our third child was a lovely four-year-old named Sopilla, the child of Thai refugees. English was her second language and she was far from fluent in it, but she too was a sweet girl who quickly became part of the group. Weeks turned to months, and these three new arrivals became a part of our family. Samantha's tantrums settled down; Sylvia gained six pounds and grew some hair; Sopilla learned to speak English and stole the hearts of the family that would ultimately adopt her.

All three were children before they were foster children, and they wanted and needed the same things all children do. They needed to snuggle in for stories, have cookies and milk every afternoon, and watch for rainbows behind the barn.

My new girls were benefiting from the experience I gained from earlier children. I now could do a better job managing Samantha's tantrums because of what I had learned from Sara. Helping Lucy move to the Malloys' made it easier to help Sopilla move on and attach to her new adoptive family. Working with the school system to address Dan's special educational needs provided the foundation for getting a school plan in place for Sylvia. When I talked with the girls' therapists, I now knew what to ask and what information they would find helpful.

I was honored when, in 1996, Bruce and I were selected as our area office's Foster Parents of the Year. I continued to serve as a liaison to all the state's foster parents, a position offered only to experienced foster parents. My job was to provide guidance and support to foster parents in crisis, but since I was still in crisis myself from time to time, I felt a little odd about it. I found that the extended contact with social workers and my peers added a fresh dimension to the work I was doing. I began to do some writing and public speaking about foster care and continued to co-lead the training classes for prospective foster families.

I still hate cocktail-party small talk, but when asked what I do, the answer comes more easily. "I do some writing and some teaching," I say, "but my important job is being a foster mother."

E p i l o g u e

❖

People still ask me how I stand it. How can I tolerate the misery and the hopelessness of it all? How can I cope with the drug addicts and the prostitutes and the pedophiles and the crazy people? "Doesn't it scare you?" they want to know. "Wouldn't you rather teach again or sell towels, for goodness' sake? Anything but continue to do what you do?" The truth is, there isn't anything I'd rather do. I think keeping a home and raising up children is a good and noble calling. I say I am a foster parent with my head held high. It's hard work and not for the faint of heart. It is sometimes a job for a warrior.

My older children were home for dinner not long ago. Bruce and I looked around the crowded table, so proud of who they have each become. Young Bruce is a single father, raising two small children by himself and doing a wonderful job. His children are bright, beautiful, and happy. Nathan speaks with such affection and maturity about the boys he counsels in a residential program for disturbed adolescents; it's hard to believe he is still in his early twenties. Not long ago I asked him what happened to his new winter coat. He blushed when he admitted that he had given it to a homeless man he found rummaging in a Dumpster. Ben writes to us each week and tells us about his missionary work. He possesses a gentleness and a sensitivity that touch everyone he meets. He'll be home next year and hopes to become a kindergarten teacher. Neddy is in college and drawn to social work and psychology. Angie, the little girl who came to us with such angry eyes and poor prospects, was recently voted Winter Carnival Queen, an honor based not just on her beauty but on her community volunteer work. She too plans to pursue a degree in social work. Karen deals with her multiple disabilities with grace and courage. What parent could hope for more?

I still hear from some of my former foster children from time to time. The news is not as bad as I feared it could be. After a few rough years bouncing around from shelter to shelter, Dan was accepted into a program designed to meet the needs of adolescent boys with developmental delays and mental health issues. He will probably never live independently, but he has a life and friends. He visits with his mother every month, and that relationship remains important to him. Sara, too, is doing better than might be expected. She remains in residential care and has managed to make it home. Although not ready for the intimacy of a family, she is making progress in putting the shadows of her childhood behind her. Lucy still writes to Angie and Neddy, and I speak often to her mother. She does well in school and is an outstanding athlete. She has brought great joy to her adoptive parents.

There have been some improvements in the social service system. Foster parents are better trained and supervised than they were when Bruce and I began. The improved training has led to a more empowered group who recognizes our obligation to advocate for the children in our care. During the good fiscal times of the late nineties, social worker caseloads were reduced to more manageable numbers, and real work was done to strengthen and support needy families. Recently, though, budget surpluses have disappeared. One by one, the supporting social programs that poor families so desperately need have been defunded. Social workers have been laid off, and once again, the remaining workers have caseloads that ensure only crisis management. One thing that hasn't changed in thirteen years is that in hard times budgets are balanced on the backs of children and the poor.

Another thing that hasn't changed is the children. The ghosts of the injured babies that Sara and Danny and Lucy once were still look at me through the eyes of each new child who comes to my home. Occasionally, after a bad day, I consider my life and think about doing something else. I think wistfully of pensions and sick days and conversations with people who don't eat oatmeal with their fingers. I have even given away the baby clothes and dismantled the crib, but doing so virtually guarantees that some fifteen-year-old will give birth to a baby she can't begin to take care of, and so I end up going out to replace everything.

I have stated repeatedly that I am absolutely through adopting. Six kids feels like a big enough family, and now my children are old enough to allow me to glimpse a future where the sandbox is empty and the tire swing hangs still. But that future feels hollow to me—too light and too empty. My imagination always leads me to another child who will need a home. I can always hear the siren's song.

For a reader's group guide to this book, please visit:

www. penguinputnam.com/guides

Acknowledgments

I would not have attempted this project without the unwavering belief of my husband, Bruce, that I was perfectly capable of pulling it off.

My good friend B. J. Roach convinced me there was a story to tell.

My children, cursed with a technologically impaired mother, typed, edited, cut and pasted, formatted, and otherwise rescued me from the clutches of my first computer.

My agent at Curtis Brown, Maureen Walters, has been a gift to an inexperienced writer. Her enthusiasm gave me the drive to turn an idea into a manuscript.

My editor at Jeremy Tarcher, Wendy Hubbert, has taken me gently by the hand and led me through this process. Her combination of wisdom, inspiration, humor, and unequivocal dedication has kept me motivated through many tough stretches.

Thank you also to Allison Sobel at Jeremy Tarcher, Joanna Durso at Curtis Brown, and my instructor, Stanley Wiater, at the University of Massachusetts.

About the Author

Kathy Harrison has been a foster parent to almost a hundred children. In 1996 she and her husband were named Massachusetts Foster Parents of the Year, and in 2002 they received the prestigious Goldie Foster Award. A frequent public speaker, Harrison lives with her husband, three biological sons, and three adoptive daughters in western Massachusetts.

Kathy Harrison with her husband, Bruce, and daughters Angie and Karen.

(Photo courtesy of DAILY HAMPSHIRE GAZETTE)